THE PRIESTHOOD

THE PRIESTHOOD

by

KARL RAHNER

Translated by Edward Quinn

HERDER AND HERDER

1973
Herder and Herder
1221 Avenue of the Americas, New York, N.Y. 10020

English translation © 1973 by Sheed and Ward Ltd. First
published 1973 by Sheed and Ward Ltd., London, England

Original Edition: *Einübung Priesterlicher Existenz*, Verlag Herder
KG Freiburg im Breisgau, 1970

Nihil Obstat: John M. T. Barton STD LSS *Censor*
Imprimatur: David Norris *Vicar General*
Westminster: 27 September 1972

Library of Congress Catalog Card Number: 72-94304
ISBN: 07-073791-6

Printed in Great Britain by W & J Mackay Limited Chatham

CONTENTS

CONTENTS

PREFACE

The crisis which the priest has to endure today, in his self-understanding and way of life, is only partly the result of changing social structures. Even if we don't underestimate the extent to which the former image of the priest – his prestige among the people of God and in society generally – was sociologically conditioned, there still remains much to be clarified about the origins of this situation.

Is the church's self-understanding as transformed by Vatican II the cause of this crisis of the priesthood? Is it a consequence also of the fact that we have no great regard for "authority"? Is it due to the present situation, to modern social mobility, which makes it advisable to choose a type of calling rather than a particular occupation? Can the priestly vocation be put under the heading of "social worker"? Is the crisis of the priesthood a result of the world becoming more worldly, of increasing secularisation, of the way in which love of God is reduced to purely human fellow-feeling? Must we regard this situation as the result of an historicist, but unhistorical outlook on the church, romanticising the primitive church as a beginning and giving it undogmatically an absolute value? Is it a symptom of the "end of modern times", of the end of a still metaphysical age, which is being dissolved by cybernetics and computers? Is it simply a sign of the general decline of deeper faith and the will to believe?

Something of what might be said about *these* problems, I have said elsewhere.[1]

In this book we are not concerned with theory, but with the practice of the priestly life; it is a question of "mystagogy", of initiation into the mystery of what "priesthood" is about. The book has emerged out of retreat conferences given to candidates for ordination in 1961. That is why the train of thought of the *Exercises* is constantly to be seen. Nevertheless, these conferences are essentially different from what I wrote in my book of meditations on St Ignatius' *Spiritual Exercises*.[2] Practice in the priestly life is not in the first place a matter of cursory reading or of study, but of reflection and meditation. These conferences are meant to stimulate a deeper understanding and a more devout acceptance of the priestly way of life.

Something also must be said about the image of the priest which can be seen in the background. This retreat was given in 1961, that is, before the council, before the reflections on church, ministry, and people of God, had been worked out in the *Constitution on the Church*, and the *Decrees on the Bishops' Pastoral Office*, on *Priestly Formation*, and on the *Ministry and Life of Priests*. Hence it will be seen that the general trend of the conferences is on traditional lines. Many a priest today will rightly ask what is the point of putting the old ideas into practice. What is the point of the old at all,

[1] For instance in *Knechte Christi*, Freiburg, 1968[2]; "Der theologische Ansatzpunkt für die Bestimmung des Wesens des Amtspriestertum" and "Theologische Reflexionen zum Priesterbild von heute und morgen" in *Schriften zur Theologie* IX, Einsiedeln, 1970, pp 366–394; "Die Zukunft der Kirche hat schon begonnen" in *Handbuch der Pastoraltheologie* IV, Freiburg, 1969, pp 744–759.

[2] *Betrachtungen zum ignatianischen Exerzitienbuch*, Munich, 1965.

now that the new is coming to be? But, quite apart from the evidence of continuity – which is by no means superfluous for developments in the church – tradition can be an important criterion; it can help to separate what is truly modern from what is merely fashionable; it can rouse the power of discernment of spirits, but it can also force a confrontation which may perhaps reveal what is so violently defended as belonging to tomorrow to be really of the day before yesterday. The future can fulfil its promise only when it is aware of its origins.

Anyone who is put off by details of this past form of the priesthood can still practise in these meditations the spirit of a truly priestly way of life, whatever this may look like in the concrete: the spirit of commitment, courage for self-criticism (which of course must come before criticism of others), the venture of faith, even though the actual shape of its realisation is not known, selfless service to one's neighbour, and – finally – love. Whether the priest of the future does justice to the claim of christian love, will be just as decisive for him as it was for his priestly forbears. Even if a number of positions maintained in this book have been modified in other writings of mine on the priesthood, there is no need to alter anything as long as it is a question of the essential claim of christianity and the priesthood: to be at the service of love among men and thus of the coming of God's kingdom.

Munich, December 1969.   Karl Rahner

1 EXPERIENCE OF GOD AND IMAGE OF GOD

Ignatius of Loyola lived at a time when God's existence was on the whole simply taken for granted, no matter what a person's religious outlook might be. This is not the case today. Not only because many people profess to be atheists, not only because there is a militant, state-organised atheism with its parties everywhere in the world, but also because we are all living at a time that makes a kind of atheism possible and provides scope for its existence.

The atmosphere in which we are living is one where God is felt or at least assumed to be remote. This atmosphere is not outside us and around us. What makes itself felt in this atmosphere and what takes on concrete historical, political and social palpability in this avowed atheism lies in a certain sense within ourselves.

If we were to deny this, if we were to act as if it were not so, it would not be because we are the people who have a stronger, more genuine belief in God, but because we were merely repressing something and thus injuring ourselves. Of course we don't need to ask: is there a God? Of course we cannot really think of anything more obvious. But the feeling that God is infinitely above us, that it is difficult to think and to be sure that we know something about him, the feeling that it is not so obvious that we are able to appeal to him and even say to him, "Abba, Father" (Rom. 8:15):

4

this feeling too is something we cannot escape. Only when we allow for it, only when we face it, can we expect our relationship to God, truly realised in a correct and christian way in the Spirit of God, to be really what it ought to be today.

We too as christians, as priests, are bound, with mankind today, to bear, to suffer to the end the want of God, God's apparent remoteness, God's silence, his ineffable mystery, in order to be in any position to have a fraternal understanding for the people of our time. That is why the place in the *Exercises* for such a meditation is before the *Foundation*. Not as theoretical, metaphysical proofs of God's existence, but in the form of an introduction, first of all realising primarily and originally the basic element of our relationship to God, before we ask what God wants of us, before we acknowledge ourselves as sinners before him, before we turn to him in this moral sense.

That he exists, that he surrounds us – so to speak – everywhere, that we can nowhere and never really escape him, that we affirm him once again when we seek him in pain and anguish, that he perhaps comes upon us at the very moment when we were thinking we would never find him again: all these features of a theological maieutic we ought to know much better than in fact we do.

1. *Experience of God*

When we think of God, abstract and difficult as it perhaps must be for human reflexion, we are asking ourselves where and how the right concept of God is really to be found.

You all know that the transcendental relatedness of

5

man's whole intellectual existence in knowing and loving, in the experience of dread and fear in face of death and so on, is one of the most essential basic features of human existence. We do not begin to have something to do with God only when we explicitly name him, when our knowledge of God acquires a conceptual and thematic structure. This latter is necessary and salutary, it is God's grace. It is then that we speak of God, form a concept and mould this concept, that we fill out this one concept with a thousand names and statements: all this is necessary, good and right. And even now, when we talk about God, we can do so only by forming words about him, by working out ideas, by being conscious of the reality of God in thematic form. But presumably you are aware that this is the secondary – but not, for that reason, unimportant – mode of the original relationship to God, and that this secondary relationship of thematic conceptuality to God is sustained and remains sustained by a previous, unthematic, transcendental relatedness of our whole intellectuality to the incomprehensible Infinite.

In the light of all this it is clear that the genuine, concretely (and existentially) realised relationship to God ought not merely to bring out and fulfil more precisely the objective-conceptual themes about God, but ought also previously and simultaneously to deepen, invigorate and bring to the fore this primal – in the most profound and necessary sense, "subjective" – ontological and transcendental relationship to God.

This however does not at all mean indulging in clever talk about these sublime things. For this again would simply not be the primal, transcendental relationship to God himself, but something secondary – in fact, merely talk about this relationship. But how then can we bring out this primal relationship to God? How must we really make it active so that we feel ourselves sustained and encompassed by God so to speak from behind and from the very depths of being? When we think of God, when we fill out our concepts of God, make them more complex, enrich their content, how do we really manage to observe that we are again living on a more primitive relationship to God and on its realisation? How do we see that we remain encompassed by God, that all these concepts are in fact merely a pointer to that primal relationship to God, which of course is always dependent also on this thematic objectivation? All this in fact remains obscure. We have to admit that we theologians and we catholics of today, in spite of all our talk about God, possess and practise really very little hermeneutic and maieutic for this more primitive experience of God given in the very roots of existence.

If what philosophy has said about this original structure of man in his intellectuality is true, then evidently such experiences must occur. Be still for once. Don't try to think of so many complex and varied things. Give these deeper realities of the spirit a chance now to rise to the surface: silence, fear, the ineffable longing for truth, for love, for fellowship, for God. Face loneliness, fear, imminent death! Allow such ultimate, basic human experiences to come first. Don't go talking about them, making up theories about them, but simply endure these basic experiences. Then in fact something like a primitive awareness of God can emerge. Then perhaps we cannot say much about it; then what we "grasp" first of all about God appears to be nothing, to be the absent, the nameless, absorbing and suppressing all that can be expressed and conceived.

If we do not learn slowly in this way to enter more and more into the company of God and to be open to him, if we do not constantly attempt to reflect in life primitive experiences of this kind – not deliberately intended or deliberately undertaken – and from that point onwards to realise them more explicitly in the religious act of meditation and prayer, of solitude and the endurance of ourselves, if we do not develop such experiences, then our religious life is and remains really of a secondary character and its conceptual-thematic expression is false; then we talk of God as if we had already slapped him on the shoulder – so to speak – and, in regard to men, we feel that we are God's supervisors and more or less his equals: the result is that, for all our preaching, we ultimately lack credibility for the men of today and for those who really count. Whenever piety is directed only by an ingenious, complicated intellectuality and conceptuality, with highly complicated theological tenets, it is really a pseudo-piety, however profound it seems to be.

Once again, however, consider for example the situations in which man is brought back to this basic experience of God. Somewhere, someone seems to be weeping hopelessly. Someone "packs it in" and knows – if he is now silent, if he is now patient, if he now gives in – that there is nothing more that he could seize on, on which he could set his hopes, that this attitude is worth-while. Someone enters into a final

8

solitude where no one accompanies him. Someone has the basic experience of being stripped even of his very self. A man as spirit in his love for truth reaches – so to speak – the frontier of the absolute, about which he has no longer anything to say, which sustains and is not sustained: that absolute which is there even though we cannot reach out and touch it, which – if we talk about it – is again concealed behind our talk as its ground. Someone experiences joy, not knowing where it begins and ceases, for which there appears to be no solid reason, which even seems to have no object. Someone does not really seize on, but is seized by, a final loyalty. There is a time when object, ground and horizon, and all that we see in these, merge – so to speak – into one another. Wherever these things happen, God is really already present and available to man.

All that man has then to say of this God can never be more than a pointer to this primitive experience of God. If someone says that this is mysticism, then it is in fact mysticism and then this very factor of mysticism belongs to God. But it is not mysticism in the specific sense: it is the obviousness of being encompassed absolutely by God at the moment of a man's whole awakening to mental existence. These things remain banal for us; this primitive, nameless and themeless experience is apparently wholly repressed and buried by our daily routine, by all that we otherwise have to do with men and things. This primal religious relationship to God can be buried again even through our theological, ascetic and pious chatter. All this proves indeed how · much we must constantly struggle in a more genuine, more religious life to set free and constantly dig out this primal relationship to God; but it proves precisely how primitive and deeply rooted is man's relationship to God and proves how much this primal relationship really matters.

Up to a point we ought to be able to show an atheist that the very fact of denying God is itself an affirmation of his existence and that this is not merely a question of formal logic, but a veritable realisation of a man's genuine, vital, concrete existence. This much has to be presupposed if what we still want to say about God is to make sense at all. What remains to be said really brings us back every time to what we have just touched on. It should only encourage us to awaken in ourselves this primitive experience of God, the experience of course of God as the ineffable and incomprehensible.

2. *Images of God*

Think of the false images of God that are found everywhere and therefore also in us.

It is all very odd. We human beings recognise the faults of others, their stupidity, their obtuseness, their cowardliness, their narrow-mindedness, their sentimentality, their traumata, their twisted feelings, their inferiority complexes. But how difficult it is to admit the same things in ourselves, to say: What I see in others is presumably in me too; presumably I am as little inclined as these others are – with their irritability, their complexes, their finiteness, which I know – to recognise myself as I really am and face the cracks in my own nature.

This observation holds too in regard to the narrow, constricted, untrue and ready-made images of God which men always set up to a certain extent as idols and thus shut out the nameless God who simply cannot be pinned down in shape and form, in an image. God transfixed in a concept, the God of the parsons is a God who doesn't exist. But don't we too often have an idol and don't we worship it when we turn religion, faith, the church, the message of Jesus Christ, from what it ought to be into a profession? This amounts to identifying with God ourselves and the world which we ourselves want to uphold and defend. Then God is really never more than a high-sounding word behind which we ourselves are masquerading, God transfixed in a concept as compared with the God who is constantly and increasingly experienced as a living, infinite, incomprehensible, ineffable reality and person: this God is one of those idols which presumably we may also constantly discover in ourselves.

The child's sweet, kind God is another idol. The narrowminded God of the pharisee obedient only to the law is yet another. The God we think we know by contrast with the God of incomprehensible love, love that is harsh and able to kill; the God taken for granted by so-called "good christians", who behave as if they could not understand the atheist's anxiety and uncertainty and as if the latter were merely stupid or malicious: this self-evident God of the good christians is also an idol of which we must beware. God – least of all the true God – is not a collective title for religion. In the religion of the Vedas we can see most clearly how all priestly activity, religion with all its machinery, can become so inflated, so autonomous, that religion ends by giving its stamp to God instead of God defining religion.

Something like this really can happen to us. Let us ask where the idols, the false concepts of God, are in our own personal piety. If we think that everything ought to make sense, to be palpable; if we think that things ought to go well for us, that everything in our life should always be crystal-clear; if we think, with the aid of a manual of moral theology or with any other concepts, norms, principles – no matter how true, how correct – we could so shape our life that it would run absolutely smoothly; if we think that God must be at our disposal as long as and because we serve him; if we think it isn't right that things should go badly; if this is how we think, then behind these cherished illusions there is a false image of God and this is what we serve. If these images are shattered by God himself and his life, by his guidance and providence, then one thing should be clear from the beginning: what is disappearing is not God, but an idol.

3. *The true God*

Let us ask ourselves what we know of this true God. In this respect, I must again recall what I said at first, when we were talking about the correct concept of God, of the God we do not grasp but who grasps us, whom we do not sustain but who sustains us. For our primal experience is not in fact of thinking of God, of knowing him, but of being grasped by him and known by him. My knowing, my loving, my longing, my fear, are already sustained from the very beginning by an incomprehensibility which in fact is called God; and indeed it is only when this primitive experience of God is somehow present in a more vital way through talking about God that this very talk of God makes sense, only then does reflection on God also acquire a deeper meaning. This is what we mean when we speak of the true God.

We mean by God, as Vatican I puts it, he who is ineffably exalted above all that is or can be thought of outside himself. We mean the God beyond our mind; we mean the God who is also "greater than our heart" (1 Jn 3:20), in such a way that this power overwhelming our heart is also the source of both our deepest grief and our greatest bliss. We mean – if we may speak in this way at all – the God who is infinite in all his attributes.

Think of his knowledge and wisdom, his power, his truth, his truthfulness, his fidelity, his goodness, his beauty, his eternity, his immensity, his ubiquity. Think of his freedom, his justice, his mercy; remember that "God" means just what man cannot say, that blazing reality which is and remains for us the absolute mystery, mystery most of all when we see him face to face for all eternity. Remember that it is God who once again sustains our knowledge when we know him; remember that God is the very word for that which marks our freedom in its ultimate, autonomous independence and yet does not belong to us. That God is the very name for the fact that something can surpass itself and that this power of self-transcendence, by being effective in us and becoming – so to speak – our own innermost strength, is precisely the power that must be acknowledged as what we are not.

Remember that God is simply the incomprehensible. That is how he is the eternal, personal, knowing, self-possessing primal cause of our existence. He is the personal God who is absolutely identical with his freedom, so that we cannot – so to speak – get behind this freedom of God and cannot seriously attempt to get the measure of his freedom by making a concrete comparison with some being that can be distinguished from him.

Think what it means when we say that God lives, God sees me, continually and forever. Think what it means when we say that God is active, he sustains me, he knows beginning and end, he brings about my destiny, he takes me seriously, he continually establishes me in my proper reality; he sends me away from him and by that very fact holds me to him; he makes me a free being, even in regard to himself, and by that very fact is my lord; he is closer to me than I am to myself and by that very fact he is infinitely distant from me.

Think what it means that God loves me. Don't think that this proposition, as it is understood here by christian faith, is a philosophical statement. It is the innermost experience of our existence, but – precisely because it is the innermost experience of our life – it is already sustained by his infinite grace. God loves me. What a tremendous thing this is when I know what is finite and infinite, what is limited and unlimitable; when I know that the Absolute loves me, that is, even in his own being and freedom and through these, he is such that he grasps me, has made my nothingness a factor in his own life, has given himself to me in the innermost, free unrelatedness and inwardness of his person, in what we call grace. All this is true even if I don't know it, even if I don't think of it, even though the narrow space of my being is felt in some way to be empty, narrow and small at the very point where it is inundated by God's infinity. All this is said when we say that God loves us.

We have said nothing. And if you or I, if we, imagine that something has been said, we are deceiving ourselves. For, as the fourth Lateran Council says, no sort of similarity can be perceived in him which is not intersected by a deadly – and for that very reason lifegiving – still greater dissimilarity. But this is just how God is to be named, just how these things are to be understood: *Latens Deitas*, which in this incomprehensibility of its eternal mystery has given itself into our heart. *Adoro te devote, latens Deitas.*

2 MAN AND "THE OTHER THINGS"

It is useful to meditate again and again on the great classical texts of the *Exercises*. They will stand up to it. They don't need to be replaced by something else. There are great documents of christianity, of its spiritual doctrine and its theology, which admittedly rank below the texts of scripture, but which are nevertheless imperishable. We shall therefore take the great fundamental meditations of the *Exercises* as they present themselves, without attempting to embellish them or replace them by anything else. What is said then by way of introduction and marginal observation to the texts themselves, is of course never the really important thing either in comparison with the text or in comparison with what is to be considered in it. For what is to be considered in these meditations is always the unity of our own individual and personal existence and these truths of faith; the synthesis of our own situation with what is said here means facing these texts with all that we are in our decisive situation before God, which we have sought, prayed for, hoped for, and patiently expected.

1. *Modern anthropocentrism*

Before considering the individual texts it may be useful to reflect, with some surprise, on the fact that in this first section such a grandiose anthropocentrism is developed that the *Foundation* must be regarded philosophically and theologically as one of the great, basic texts of modern times. It is not true that we christians, in the last resort and in our innermost understanding, ought to consider this time in which we are living today as a time that is not in harmony with christianity and its message. On the contrary, we can conceive this so-called modern age in what it is ultimately striving for and thinking entirely as becoming theologically and practically aware of what christianity really is.

St Ignatius begins with the word *el hombre* (23)[1] and ends with the *Suscipe* (234) in exactly the same existential, philosophical and theological terms, since man sees himself here again as freedom and this freedom is given priority before the three powers of memory, understanding and will. We are then in fact faced with the feeling of modern times in its utter and obvious simplicity, wholly unsurprised at itself, that feeling in which what is really the ultimate and deepest feeling of christianity becomes reflexively self-evident.

St Thomas Aquinas was the first theologian and philosopher within christianity to turn the cosmocentrism of antiquity, of the Greek mind (not of course in the technical doctrinal details, but in the philosophical basic sense) to an anthropocentrism. This is not in opposition to a theocentrism, but precisely in order also to provide scope for the conceptual expression of man's real theocentrism. Man is not a mere element in the cosmos, a tiny worm that happens to be found existing in any sort of material world: he is the one who stands before God and in regard to whom all the rest, apart

---

[1] The numbers refer to the paragraphs of the *Exercises*. The text is that of the revised edition of a translation by John Morris and others published by Burns and Oates with a preface by Henry Keane, SJ (London 1952[5]).

from himself and God, are called "the other things" (23).

This is not merely a philosophical conversion of the ancient sense of the world into the christian, but is something essentially theological: man, not the world, is what God intends. He is not an element in a world, but the world in the last resort is an element in him and for him. If this ultimate basic feeling, contrary to the Greek and also contrary to much in the conventional formulation of christian feeling, still caught up in the unchristian Greek, coincides with and is found in the ultimate basic feeling of what we call modern times, then this arises from the fact that the modern world, even when it is wholly unaware of it, or denies it, when it draws false conclusions from its basic feeling, is in reality christian.

St Ignatius is certainly not a theologian if we are speaking of theology as a reflective science, nor is he a philosopher in that sense. But he is a man who stands, in an absolutely providential way, at the beginning of a new age which cannot and must not be understood – as Romano Guardini, for instance, understood it – as coming to an end, but as always still coming to be, as always to be understood and overtaken only by christianity, by us, the narrow-minded, primitive representatives and trespassers of christianity. We still have to spell out the texts of an Ignatius.

It is not self-evident that the theme here should be of man and "the other things": that I (the individual human being) exist in an absolutely decisive way so that I can see everything else that exists, the whole world, only as the "other things", while seeing myself on the other hand as the one who is directly engaged in dialogue with God.

This conception is maintained throughout the

Exercises, as when we read that God the creator should be left to deal and communicate "immediately" (15) with his creature; when in the *Exercises* it is not a situation-ethic that is worked out, but a genuinely radical individual ethic that involves finding out in each case what is God's will for me, a will that only God himself can directly make known to me. If then Ignatius has man in mind throughout the *Exercises*, we have before us a modern sense of the world which we must again examine.

Although it strikes us almost as boring, we cannot take such a simple text too seriously. It is anything but a truism. It is not true that what is said here is simply what christendom had always known. Of course this is said and no more than this is intended. But it is said in a way that was only acquired and could only be acquired by the christianity of modern times. It is said in the light of an historical situation which is specifically that of modern times and not in fact that of a "new age" which simply passes away again, which divides off some other epoch – for example, that of the middle ages as a mere transition from antiquity to modern times. It is said in the light of a situation where a new age is beginning, which, since it is the final, unsurpassable dawn of a christianity aware of itself, can no longer simply pass away, no matter how little we know what later ages will look like, however much as creatures of historicity we shall continue to wander into realms of existence the measure of which we had not hitherto known.

2. *Man: the creature*

We are considering man as creature. "Man is created"

19

(23). If it is not to be misunderstood, this text must be understood, not as referring to Everyman, but as referring to me. Otherwise "the other things" are not clearly seen. What is meant here is "I" and no one else. It is true that there are others like me, but only in a certain sense. For each man must perceive the splendid and terrible reality, the fact that places him in isolation before God: that he is unique and exists once only.

He must do this: he cannot retreat into the mass; he cannot hide himself in that which holds always and for all. Man: this am I, completely alone, however true it is that every other one who is man must also say the same of himself. But in fact what he says of himself is simply a generalisation, but the "general" must here be heard, read, experienced and accepted in the absolute solitude of the individual, in the existence that is on each occasion "mine".

What is said here then about "man" must be understood as referring to "me". When I say "I", everything else must fall back into that circle of the "other things" in regard to which I am the unique, incommensurable one, with a partner ultimately only in God, so that when I am afraid in this uniqueness, when I feel the dizziness and dread of this loneliness, I can take refuge only in God.

The proposition, "Man is created" (23), must be read as a statement in the present tense. I have not been created once and for all in the past, but I am now the created one, my being created is something that is constantly taking place. Hence it must be said that I am the creature, now, uniquely. I am the one known to myself, that one who is directly the sole being which has this characteristic of being immediately known,

the characteristic which enables me to reach everything else. And at the same time I am the one unknown
to myself. I am being-present-to-myself, I am freedom.
"I am" means: I am inescapably; I am the appointed
beginning which cannot get back behind itself, and
this beginning is "there". If I were to kill myself, if I
were to protest against my existence, if – in Dostoyevsky's words – I "wanted to return my entry card into
this world", I would again be confirming my existence,
I would again be placed before this absolute barrier
that I am and that I am not non-existent.

To say that I exist as a creature means further that I
am finite and I know it. In me this finiteness becomes
aware of itself and here alone becomes radically finite.
I endure myself then; I know my limits, I overstep
them and at the same time keep to them. Nevertheless
I am: I am not merely appearance, not merely an
illusion; not everything about me is unreality which
could be overridden. I am as I am, inescapably as the
known-unknown, as the being become present to itself
and as that which is in control of itself, which – how
incomprehensible it really is! – is given into its own
hands.

As such however I am always the one who is directed
away from myself: I am present to myself and always
look away from myself. This towards-which-I-am is
God and we call him therefore the incomprehensible,
absolute freedom, over which we have no control.
When we say, "I am referred to God," we cannot
simply add that all is then clear, but we are basically
saying: "I am that one who, if he is really the one referred to God, can never 'become clear' to himself
about himself". For if we are those who are referred to

God, if we are men who are created, then we understand ourselves adequately, we become transparent to ourselves, only when we understand God; and this is denied the creature for all eternity, even in the beatific vision. Or, better, it is not denied us, but the bliss of eternity lies in the fact that we are dealing with a God who himself is close to us as the incomprehensible mystery, and as infinite incomprehensibility lays hold on us down to the last fibre of our being.

As priests and as the church's representatives, don't we talk about God as if everything were clear? This is lying and untruth. If we talk of God, then let us tell men straight: You must never consider your life closed, you must never think that your account has reached its final figure; you must never think that you can make yourself comfortable in the comprehensibility of your existence. Let us tell man: You must get away from the familiarity of your existence, you are travelling towards an absolute infinity of which you can never get the measure. Then let us say to man and to ourselves: All that lies before you is not the real thing, and however familiar it might be to you, however lovingly you set about making yourself at home here and assume that you can find the real thing in all this, nevertheless, because you are man knowing himself to be created by God, God himself forces you to get out, even if it is night, even if it can be endured only in an ecstasy of love that submits with blissful courage to God's incomprehensibility. For it is only when God is seen in this way that he is not seized on and apprehended, but his incomprehensibility is accepted as the blessed content of our existence; only then is it admitted that this God really rules and should rule behind our existence;

then we have said "Yes" to the incomprehensibility of our own existence – and only then have we brought to the surface what we are as creatures.

All this is not meant to be an intellectual exercise of reflection, but is what occurs in our life when we live, when we sacrifice, when we are loyal, when we die, when we celebrate the death of Christ. Here man's creatureliness comes to itself as the dawning on us of God's incomprehensibility, as God's closeness and blessedness for us. We are rooted in God, in the un-known-incomprehensible, we are rooted in the abyss of the absolute, in the abyss of God's freedom, and by accepting this we are what we ought to be. If we don't accept it lovingly, this would still permeate our exist-ence, but then as the volcanic, destructive eruption of what we are.

3. *Man's goal*
In the light of this Ignatius tells us our task and our goal: "Created to praise, reverence, and serve God our Lord, and by this means to save his soul" (23).

In the first place, you will be surprised that there is no mention of love in this text. That is all to the good. Here we read only of praise, reverence and service, so that love in a general way can be understood. For it is understood only when it forgets itself in praise, rever-ence and service. Here again we have this virile sensibility of modern man who never ventures to in-gratiate himself with God, who knows that we cannot simply enjoy God, the incomprehensible, as the euphoria of our own existence. Here is the sensibility of the really modern man who knows that we have to serve, silently, humbly, worshipping the incomprehensible, accepting with resignation and therefore with reverence the providence that is beyond our control. In all this there is true praise of God: not in our talking, but in what we do and are, in what we suffer, endure, as suffering divine things, *pati divina*, in which alone God becomes known to us.

When we read this text in its whole depth, we see that praise, reverence, service, are not something which happens incidentally, but what we are when we freely want to be what we are, when we accept ourselves. At the very point where man sees himself in this genuine, radical, christian anthropocentricism, he learns and knows that his action and his experience are not something that happens at the superficial margin of his existence, without his nature being affected by it. "The other things" are like that, but man in his freedom accepts his own nature, and this nature in the act of his freedom is impregnated down to its deepest roots with what he is, so that deed and nature enter into a synthesis which is indissoluble for all eternity. If this were not so, we would not be eternally in God's presence in what is created by God and done by us. Praise, reverence and service, therefore, are not something that we do on the side: they are what we ourselves are when we freely accept our being as what our freedom has done.

We exist as praise of God, as reverence, which keeps to itself, is aware of itself only at a distance from God, always open to God and constantly at his disposal: we are reverence when in God's service we venture timidly to be love. Task and goal therefore may not be understood in a primitive, short-sighted way as a moral norm. They are that too of course, but why?

Because we are created as praise, reverence and service of God and because this creation is not first and
last a creation for a moral task, but creation as appoint-
ment and authorisation, as inescapability, directly con-
ferred on existence abandoned to itself. Praise, reverence and service must be seen from the very beginning
as that which is given to us and for which – to our
delight and surprise – we feel that we are authorised,
as what we are permitted, as what we are, and as what
is given to be known and accepted by ourselves. This of
course necessarily means joy and bliss also: for reality
distinct from God becomes aware of itself and thereby
God comes to us. Joy grows in a transparency of existence into the incomprehensible mystery of God.

All this is then the effecting of our soul's salvation.
When Ignatius adds this, he does not mean that human
existence returns to itself as if – so to speak – it wanted
at any rate to save its skin. According to the most ele-
mentary theology – which we constantly forget in our
everyday egoism – there is only one way to save our
souls, if we mean the whole work of saving our souls:
this is love for God. But in this love man gets away
from himself without returning; he serves so that God
may be served, he praises God that God may be
praised, he is reverent so that in this reverence before
God he is forever stripped of himself: thus gaining the
soul's salvation is not the purpose of the service of God
in praise and reverence, but is already achieved in
this service of reverence and praise. And the fact that
as catholics we rightly look to the salvation of our souls
(as Ignatius does here) is – once again – nothing but
the humble acceptance and realisation of the creatureliness of the creature which learns in its existential fear

that God is God and we are not God – and thus in this concern for its soul's salvation really does once again get away from itself into the service of God.

4. *The other things*

Consider what Ignatius says about the "other things". First of all admire the anthropocentricism of the world, take seriously what you read here: "the other things were created for man's sake" (23). The whole evolution of the world (and this is true in a christian, in an Ignatian sense, before Teilhard de Chardin), the whole history of nature and the world, is one single, colossal development towards man, in whom the world as the radical making over of created things now becomes aware of itself. Otherwise what we read here would not be true.

These things tell of the grandeur of the world as our world. Think of the abundance, the riches, the diversity of this world in itself, in its entities, in its history. Think not only of the world of nature, but also of the world of historicity, the world of man. Suppose that suddenly all that the poets have said of man and his lot, of his riches, of the human problem, of the depths which man can reach, were to be brought home to you: these are "the other things". This world is the grandeur of our existence because we must constantly take it anew into our heart – and it is the burden and menace of our existence. This world is continually coming to be in our individual lot and in that of mankind as a whole and it is going to God, whether we like it or not. This world, these "other things" thrust themselves upon us, delighting us, but also tormenting and killing.

If we want to do justice at all to this text, we ought

to ask: What have these "other things" to do with our immediacy to God? It isn't easy to answer this. The terse simplicity of the text might tempt us to see this relationship to God on the part of the creature directly related to God too simply in the light of these "other things on the face of the earth". These things are not merely the veil of the sacred; they are not, as the liturgy perhaps too simply expresses it, earthly things to be despised while we love the heavenly: *terrena despicere et amare caelestia*. These things cannot simply be passed over. No immediacy to God could involve simply the elimination of these other things.

All this sounds simple and obvious. But enormous theoretical and practical problems are concealed in this simple assertion that Ignatius never thought that these "other things on the face of the earth" could be simply left out or passed over in a flight from the world; that, always and everywhere, because they truly are and are not non-existent, they signify mediatorship between God and ourselves and yet cannot abolish or set aside this immediacy to God who is greater than us. They are not the important thing that might be despised; they are the mediating factor and yet they are not simply God's gift itself, for God gives us himself. They are the sacrament of God, the effective sacrament of God, in which God gives us himself. Their position between God and us can ultimately be described somehow only dialectically through the concept of sacrament, the Chalcedonian concept of *asunchutos kai adiairetos* (DS 302); it merges therefore ultimately into a mystery, which is mastered to some extent only in the concreteness of existence.

If we were to take the usual view and say that, for

27

Ignatius, "the other things" are merely means, then we would have to say from an anthropocentric standpoint that our fellow man, loved by God, is not simply a means: man has not only a world around him, but a world that is with him. We should then have to say: God in his *Logos* became man for ever and we cannot adequately describe the meaning and importance of this humanity of the eternal *Logos* itself if we see him merely as a means; for a means would be disposed of, but the *Logos* become flesh remains for eternity. If we said that the other things are only means, we would deny the fact that there is an eternity of the flesh, a transfiguration of the world, and that this world is so filled with God that it gives God to us. Therefore it is obvious too, as Ignatius says, that man has to make use of these things.

But what are we to call this mediating relationship of reality? We could perhaps say that it is the mediating of immediacy to God. This is not a clear formula. Obviously the concrete relationship to the world around and, with us, to the other things, if life is lived in a christian way, is not dependent on our having an elegant and deeply meaningful formula for it. But the mastering of christian existence, as it would have to be in the true, higher synthesis of flight from the world and being in love with the world, is to some extent dependent on our seeing in theological terms how and what the "other things on the face of the earth" really are for us. At any rate, we see that this relationship to God, and therefore also to things, to ourselves and to other persons, is always one of love for God and the world, and a love that continues to increase while remaining always free.

Ask yourself now how to combine into one statement this unity of making use of things and getting free from them. For ultimately there must of course be *one* way of using and becoming free from these things. Things can be both used and renounced as required when increasing love for God, who is greater than us, is freely active in the world, in his creation: for then both can be really combined in one, in the light of the ultimate, basic attitude. In the last resort, things do not hinder us in the service of God; at most, they become an obstacle when I fail to give a greater and increasing love to God.

All this is perhaps a very theoretical reflection, a reflection which might mislead you into overlooking what really matters here: that I am asked each time in the whole concrete situation of my existence whether I truly see myself as God's creature in this existence of mine or whether I am still closing my eyes to what I am, to what I inescapably am; this would mean that, out of the world or delivered up to the world, I am abandoned to myself instead of surrendering – not in theory and feeling, but in my whole life – in service and praise, in reverence and love, to the mystery we call God and worship under that name.

3 NATURE AND ACHIEVEMENT OF INDIFFERENCE

In the second part of the *Foundation* Ignatius draws from the first the conclusions: "It is therefore necessary that we should make ourselves indifferent to all created things, in so far as it is left to the liberty of our freewill to do so, and is not forbidden; in such sort that we do not for our part wish for health rather than sickness, for wealth rather than poverty, for honour rather than dishonour, for a long life rather than a short one; and so in all other things, desiring and choosing only those which most lead us to the end for which we were created" (23).

1. *Indifference as basic structure of mental life*

Before we consider this foundation as a moral requirement, as an ascetic norm for ourselves, it may be a good thing first of all to see this *indifferentia* as in fact belonging to the essential structure of mental life. For if man is always the one who grasps the finite, individual thing in his knowledge and in his freedom in a movement directed basically towards absolute reality, towards absolute truth and goodness, in the necessary realisation of his mental life he always transcends the individual thing, he dissociates himself from it, he sets the finite, individual thing against a broader horizon, he rises above it, makes himself independent of it: he is "indifferent" in regard to the individual thing. We might say: The transcendence of human mental life in

knowledge and freedom is itself that natural and supernatural basic indifference which is written into man's
nature, and in face of which he alone has to answer the
question whether or not he identifies himself in his
freedom with this indifference of his nature, which is
achieved at the roots of his mental life. Whenever we
know the finite as finite, the good as provisional, the
individual as contingent; whenever we tell the small
truth of an affirmative judgment in virtue of affirming
absolute truth; when we are free, we are in fact saying
that, in the depth of our being, as ground of our being,
there is an indifference in face of the finite, individual
thing and that this is disowned if we do not become
indifferent, that we are in fact in the process of destroying our own existence.

2. *Attainment of indifference*

Ignatius says it is necessary to make ourselves indifferent. What we are – for the being that we are, which is
aware of itself, freely disposes of itself – is also our task.
The indifference of our nature is the essential task of
our life, it has to be undertaken. We must dispose ourselves for indifference, make ourselves indifferent. This
means first of all that, in all that we are, in learning,
enduring, going on loving, we must affirm, accept,
develop openness and becoming open for the greater
reality. We must keep ourselves open for what is
greater, we must want to be the transcendence that we
are. We never come to the end, nowhere can we finally
rest, we are those who are open to the infinity of God –
and this we must want to be. Not only in theory, but
in the actuality of the small, bitter reality of our life.
This is really difficult. We fall for the individual thing,

we want to turn the particular object that we can grasp into our God, the idol of our life; we don't want to be driven out of the place where we are settled; we become mediocre; the absurd triviality of our normal life appears to us as something great, important and significant; we cannot permit anything to be taken from us, we cannot make a sacrifice, we cannot recognise the small things as small or the transitory as transitory.

Indifference as a task means first of all becoming open for the greater reality, ultimately for God. But this is not something we can take for granted, something that comes about of itself. The truth is that indifference as part of the essential structure of our mental life, if it is to be integrated into personal freedom, will be met with a mysterious resistance, which can be overcome only painfully and through the experience of something like death. There is, after all, the mystery of guilt, of sin, of egoism.

Perhaps we do not see how this sort of thing is possible; we do not know where this resistance to the indifference that belongs to our nature as transcendent really comes from; but this attempt to dispose ourselves for indifference, this forsaking of self and finite reality, this resignation, are opposed within ourselves by a deep, radical egoism. This must be overcome. Our task then is not something simple and obvious, but painful: it means something like a continual dying in the midst of our life.

The mastery of indifference, the constantly renewed effort to make ourselves indifferent, is difficult, hard, continually rouses a protest from something within us that claims to be what really matters. We are constantly under the impression – false and deceptive of course – that some particular thing in our life would make us free, exhilarated, blissfully happy; we are continually identifying ourselves with some particular thing, we don't want to transcend this, to get away from it and sacrifice it. Indifference is a task which seems to mean at least sacrifice, self-denial, renunciation and death. Each of us must ask himself where and in regard to what reality he must face this experience.

This death of sinful egoism involves courage for indifference, the courage to accept our own nature; it is in reality life lived with the incarnate Word of God. For he is pure receptivity, pure reception from the Father and pure return of reality to the Father. And he, who became man, in the dimension of his human life, receives the glory of his Father through death. Hence this indifference, apparently so philosophical, at the roots of our engraced existence and as the task of our liberty, is a sharing in living the life of Christ.

This indifference, then, is always a mystery. For in this indifference we turn from what we understand to the incomprehensible, from what we are enjoying to what is promised, from the present to the future, from what we can grasp to what we cannot grasp. It is an indifference in which a person declares that he will really take his stand solely in the unfathomable depths of God, that everything else – however much it is willed by God and therefore also to be affirmed, accepted, enjoyed and loved by us – is indeed always only that which in its finiteness rises out of an infinite depth and that which must always be hidden again in the greater and incomprehensible reality of God himself. This adaptation to indifference is therefore also a task freshly imposed each day.

We never are indifferent, we are constantly coming to be so. For whatever confronts us freshly and unforeseen, as what we experience in the odyssey of our mental, religious and christian life, is precisely a new and unforeseen reality and must always be surmounted freshly and in a different way. This is the constantly new task, the constantly new surprise, the constantly new pain, the daily dying with Christ and also the splendour of our existence: we never come to the end of it. The God who is greater than we are is always revealing himself anew in what we have surmounted, in what we have come to terms with, in what we have freely accepted.

3. *Dimensions of the exercise of indifference*

Ignatius also outlines the basic dimensions, the ultimate, essential dimensions for the exercise of this indifference, when he speaks of health and sickness, wealth and poverty, honour and dishonour, long life and short. Three dimensions are given.

There is first of all the corporality of existence in health and sickness: the biological, instinctive element, this inner self-assertion of bodily existence, all the impulses and instincts of our inner man. Over against this, we should have a ground in God; we should be men who, however much we accept everything and thereby fulfil ourselves, are indifferent to all this: that is we have already secured everything in the God who is greater than all.

The second dimension is self-assertion over against our personal environment, in regard to the values which are explicitly grasped in intellectual-conceptual forms: honour and dishonour, wealth and poverty.

This self-assertion too, over against the environment, should be encompassed and surmounted by indifference.

The final and third factor, described as long life or short, is really the totality of existence as such. We don't belong even to ourselves. Our freedom in regard to ourselves, if it is properly exercised, consists precisely in putting ourselves at the disposal of another, so that we ourselves simply and freely accept ourselves as under control, as not having roots in ourselves, as not looking to ourselves, and in this sense are indifferent to ourselves. We perceive that we gain a footing only at the point where we break away from ourselves; that we are in possession of ourselves only when we get away from ourselves and not otherwise.

These are abstract terms. Try in this retreat to apply these theoretical reflections in practice. Ask yourself where in your life does the actual task of your indifference lie? Where, in view of what, towards what is indifference required? Since Ignatius himself distinguishes between what is left to our free choice and what is not only morally, but also objectively, ontologically, outside its control, that which must be surmounted by this transcendence of indifference in our life and in its varied history, is in fact different for each one in his own situation.

We are constantly those who have left one thing in order to cling so much the more desperately to something else: we are never definitively indifferent. Consider the people you meet. You will be shocked to see how they fail to be indifferent, how they cling to the oddest things as if their life would be shattered without them, as if it were impossible to be happy without some particular possession. Consider the inferiority complexes of the people around you, the traumata and self-deceptions. Recognise all this as a want of indifference and say to yourself: "As the others seem to me, presumably I am also: I don't perceive my lack of indifference."

Never forget that this indifference is never something that must be present merely on the rational, conceptual surface of our freedom. There are many people who say that they renounce one thing or another, but they don't succeed in planting this indifference into the core of their being and for that reason their inner man contradicts the theoretical and explicit indifference of their superficially ascetic life. They are not indifferent. although they say they want to be.

Here of course we see that indifference is an arduous, interminable task of a lifetime, in the last resort a grace of God. Don't forget, when you ask yourself about the practical application of this requirement of indifference in your own life, that indifference is simply not an attitude of heroism, but a smiling, gentle composure, without any self-importance, completely spontaneous and natural – apart perhaps from some of life's ultimate decisions.

What does it matter in the long run whether we get through an examination or not; what does it matter in the long run whether we have a little more or a little less success, that is, whether we see more quickly or more slowly how small everything is in this human life; what does it matter in the end whether we gain a little more or a little less of what we call happiness in our brief lives: for everything passes away, everything is small? Why then do we not summon up this natural, manly, simple resignation, accepting our own unimportance?

It is easy to say this. But look for the point in your own life where this indifference becomes difficult for you. Remember that we are always in danger of having sacrificed the big things without giving up the small; remember that man is constantly in danger of offering God the greater sacrifice so that he will not demand the lesser. Remember that we often get over the greatest hurdles and fall at the smallest; remember too that modesty, ordinariness, normality, can also again be a mask, a façade, concealing a lack of indifference; remember that we can appear to be humble because we are too cowardly to expose ourselves to the great danger of being contradicted. Try really to find the point in your own life where you try to close your eyes to the indifference which is required of you; don't underestimate the indifference to small things which is required of you: for this could be precisely the Archimedean point at which a life's decision is made. Then you have grasped sufficiently the question, the prayer, the hope, the self-criticism contained in these few words which Ignatius says to you.

4. The "more"

Finally, we shall consider briefly the Ignatian "more" (23). We come back constantly to this theme of Ignatian spirituality. This much must be accepted at once: in this "more" is summed up first of all the duty which is beyond all calculation and reward, the duty of loving God with our whole heart, so that only when the whole man is utterly used up and overtaxed is he the man he has to be if he wants ultimately to find God. On the other hand of course this "more" of Ignatius is the will to a better means, to the more direct way. But these two things are both to be distinguished from one another and yet not separated from each other.

No one, no christian, without losing his soul, can really want to refuse the "more" of divine love. No christian can assert that he is always and everywhere bound to the "more" in the sense of choosing always the better means; and no christian can say that these two things have nothing to do with each other. It is as a result of this that the situation in which we have to choose, the situation in which Ignatius in the *Exercises* wants to place us, is in fact so uncanny: the greater love, absolute love, is always required of us; in regard to it, to that one thing, there are many means, many ways. None of these can be regarded as absolute. We are constantly asked which is really the way for my love, the way intended by God for me, the unique, unrepresentable, incommensurable? We have constantly to seek it afresh. We have constantly to find it. There is no road laid out in advance, no definitive way, already clearly described in the geography of universal morality. For this way of mine into the country of the priesthood I must also be constantly asking God and for him I must keep myself constantly open in indifference.

4 THE TRIPLE SIN

In our personal life, in the life of the world and in the history of the church, in our apostolate, there is the reality of sin. We have to engage in a personal struggle with it. Together with the theme of God's mercy, it is the theme of world-history, and it also represents something in our priestly task that cannot be eliminated. For we are there to convince the world of sin, of the justice and mercy of God, and to offer it – this sinful world – God's grace, which in Jesus Christ our Lord is to be victorious even over sin, so that the world's "No" remains encompassed in the greater "Yes" of God.

1. *Preliminary remarks*

Sin is a mystery. In the last resort we cannot understand how sin is possible for a creature that proceeds from the hand of God, stems only from him, containing nothing that would not attest the goodness and holiness of God. God's word assures us at least that something of this kind exists: a real "No" to God which is something other than the inevitable imperfection of the finite creature or merely a transitional stage of evolution.

Sin is sin. Sin is the incomprehensible that should not be, which does not have to be; it is what the creature can retain for itself alone, but of which it cannot be proud, in which it loses itself, in which it falls to pieces. We cannot understand sin, we cannot make it

39

an entry in our life's account now ruled off and fully explained. We can only flee from it and ask God: Lead us not into temptation and forgive us our trespasses.

Nevertheless, particularly as priests, we must constantly say that this mystery of iniquity is and remains in God's hands. Seen objectively from God's standpoint, there is no sin that could be understood in terms of dualism (ethical, if not expressly ontological). God remains Lord, also of sin. It cannot affect him, he rejects it, and yet he can permit it; he does not will it and yet it remains as part of his plan; he hates it, as scripture says, and yet, although it seeks to utter an absolute "No" to God, it cannot abolish the greater love and mercy, the holiness of God. We cannot act as if we could promote the plans of God through sin, as if we – slight, finite creatures, assigned our finite place – could survey God's plans and of ourselves find there a place for sin. We may not do evil so that God's grace may abound. Nevertheless, sin and above all sin already committed is encompassed by God, by his plan, his greater power, his love, his grace. It does not escape him. He can account for it, although it is our act; and we cannot ask him why he has permitted it, although his permission does not mean at all that we may commit sin.

Don't forget that this mystery is revealed to us in salvation history only as a factor in the unveiling of God's mercy. God tells us the abysmal depths of our sin in order to reveal to us the deeper abyss of his everlasting mercy. It is only to the extent that his mercy is made known to us that we see how hopeless our situation would be if we were to think of ourselves simply in terms of our own resources. Don't forget that the radical seriousness of our life, which is revealed in the light of the christian teaching on sin, really means the radical seriousness of God's mercy, of the God in whose mercy alone we are justified, together with our freedom; it reveals the radical seriousness of God's love which is our salvation.

Although we must further consider with Ignatius the absolute possibility of sin as the cause of final damnation and perdition for ourselves, we are also permitted to cherish a christian optimism of universal hope. This hope is not only permitted, but also required of us, as hope of course, not as knowledge; as hope and not as shrewd calculation which gets the better of God; as hope which is radically open to God's judgment and at his disposal; as hope that is genuine only if it accepts just as radically the fact that God is just, that he is holy, that he has given man such freedom that the latter is able to bring final damnation on himself even after he has been justified.

All the meditations of the first week (24–91) are always existential meditations: the person I am considering is myself, even in regard to the triple sin (51–53). In this connection, it is never ultimately a question of past sins, but of the concrete possibility of my freedom deliberately to sin, of sin that I can still commit.

The sin that I have committed and that I confess, from which I flee to God's mercy, in regard to which I believe that "God is greater than our hearts" (1 Jn 3:20), this sin has – so to speak – slipped back into God's larger plan, into his love, it is still open; in my life as a pilgrim, as someone who is encompassed by God's self-revealing mercy, it can be given a new stamp, something can really be made out of it (not from itself, but by God's power). Sin known and recognised as an accomplished fact, placed before God and his mercy, is past. It continues to exist then only as the holy shrewdness of divine love, because he is the God of mercy and can still do something with the creature's sin, as long as the creature itself does not think it has to take the initiative in making something of sin. All this presupposes that man keeps to his place: the place of obedience, the place at which man and not God stands, the place of repentance, the place of humble, obedient self-restraint, the place where man is prepared apparently to give up the greater, more glorious chances of his life in obedience to God, so that his will and not ours may be done. If the creature stands at this place or returns to it after leaving it through sin, then through the power of God's redeeming love in Jesus Christ and his cross, past sin too is changed into something again quite different. What we are really considering therefore in all these meditations here is the serious possibility of our becoming sinners.

We might presumably say that the sins which a person really, honestly admits before God are the harmless sins, perhaps (without setting out here a thesis of moral theology) even those which are not at all serious. But our situation as sinners is not thereby rendered innocuous. On the contrary: the radical threat to our existence comes from the sins we don't admit but nevertheless commit.

The moral theologians are really touching in their treatise *De Principiis*, where they write as good, innocent christians. We learn there that a grave sin can be committed only when there is a clear awareness of its sinfulness. This of course is absolutely correct in an ultimate, metaphysical sense; but this clear awareness is an awareness at the core of the person. The individual can commit sin even when he persuades himself that he is not sinning, even when he denies that he is really sinning and argues with the dialectical ingenuity of his whole being, defending and protecting himself and presenting to God an *apologia pro vita sua*.

Have you ever met many people who have certainly and clearly sinned gravely, who have betrayed their most sacred obligations, who have committed adultery, who have given up their priesthood, and who at the same time admit that they are poor, desperate, miserable sinners? No: they will defend themselves, they will blame the world, their fate, they will have a thousand reasons why in fact they can and must act just in this way; and they will maintain that God himself cannot dispute this. They will actually claim that, if they were to come before God's judgment seat, he would have to admit that he had planned the world, history, their own life, badly; he would have to admit that they were perhaps poor and weak, but certainly not common sinners, worthy of damnation, whose final end could only be in that sediment of history, in that abyss of senseless nothingness that we call hell. This they will not admit.

Nevertheless, God's word tells us that there is sin in the world. Even if I could assume that the most abandoned criminals of world history, capable indeed of anything, are really miserable creatures made so by heredity and environment, even if I were to defend the whole world, I must be prepared to admit that there is one person who cannot be defended and that he knew, although he did not want to know, although he repressed it, although he had a thousand good excusing causes: and I must have the courage to be this one.

Here of course once again there is the existential difficulty, which also is not brought out clearly enough in moral theology, that no one knows in fact whether he can say: God's grace did protect and does protect me against sin. Am I the one who is justified by the grace of God – or am I the one who is unwilling to perceive sin in his own life? It is because in the last resort we do not know this – that is, because reflection and meditation cannot assure us of it – that we have this first week of the *Exercises*.

We cannot place ourselves on the judgment seat, neither on that before which we are acquitted nor on that which damns and condemns us and convicts us of committed sin but, since we do neither the one nor the other, we capitulate before the incomprehensible God, who is justice and grace, holiness and mercy all in one, and tell him: this is what we are.

Here is the depth of our being, where we cannot reflect and where God dwells in us as the Holy Spirit, who is love's final "No" to all lovelessness and who is God's mercy. There he knows and we know who we are. But only there. We, the ones who reflect, who must up to a point give an account to ourselves and who can no more say the last word about ourselves than we can about others, we fly to God, to his mercy, and bring with us what we are. We carry our abyss into the greater abyss of God's mercy.

2. *The sin of the angels*

Let us consider first the sin of the angels (50). What Ignatius teaches us to consider in this meditation on the triple sin are not any sort of past events, but the very thing that constitutes the historically free character of the situation in which we are living: it is a meditation on the pre-history of our own existence, at least in regard to the first and second sin.

When we consider the sin of the angels, we are not thinking of the sin of a Leibnizian monad, with which we have nothing to do. The angels too belong to the world in which we live. They are the powers, the personal structural principles, of that reality which is given to us in advance as the sphere of our own existence and our own life's decision. There sin – including that of the angels – is always present. This means precisely that we must not consider the bad angels, the demons, the devils, as some kind of mysteriously stupid creatures who do absurd and wicked things in the world of the God of love. No: they commit sin just because they accomplish God's will as powers and principalities, as the internal structural principles of the particular dimensions of the world, but in an autonomous fashion, as incomprehensibly emancipated from God's greater providence. It is just here that the enticing, fascinating character of all these human dimensions of the world appears, that it looks as if all these things could only be perfected if we too were emancipated from God. Angels are factors in my existence and in a true sense equal to me.

The sin of the angels also tells us that sin is an event in the mind and not primarily in the flesh. It was in the

45

created mind at the origin of all reality that the first sin took place. There and not in the body. There in the glory of power, not in the weakness of our poverty. This means for us that the great danger of sinning lies, not at the point where we are tired, poor, weak, but at the source of our mental existence, where we become arrogant, secretive, emptied of love. It is here that the anonymous, unexpressed, and therefore the most dangerous and most monstrous aversions from God take place.

The angels' sin occurs too already within the sphere of Christ. We can readily agree with Suarez (since this is the only thing that makes sense) that the grace of the angels, their call to the triune life of God as he is in himself, was already Christ's grace, was willed by God because he willed his utterance of himself into the emptiness of the non-divine, in the flesh of Christ. From that point onwards all reality is willed and planned, the angels too as spirit-personal structural forces of the material world, of the flesh of Christ. That is why the sin of the angels is also necessarily – implicitly or explicitly – a "No" to the incarnation of the *Logos*.

The sin of the angels also shows us sin as finality. Here the life of freedom appears as that which itself creates finality. Freedom does not mean the possibility of constantly doing something else. Freedom is not the possibility of continual revision, but precisely the possibility in principle of the definitive, the unrevisable, the permanent. There already is seen the dangerous character of our freedom: of its nature it does not want the possibility of a conversion; of itself it seeks to be the deed in which man unreservedly and totally fulfils and exhausts himself and creates what is final and irrevocable, because the final, the permanent and the irrevocable, is the eternal.

Freedom is the time in which eternity comes to be, in which it creates itself. This is seen most clearly in the sin of the angels. The angels' sin then is naturally also a basic event, prior to all reflexion, in the depths of our own existence: it is an existential planted in the creaturely origin of the world, of the history of mind and matter, to which we can and must always say "No", which is always released – so to speak – through man's created freedom, which is to be surpassed, in face of which man (whether he knows or not) must always make a decision in his own freedom.

Ignatius invites us to apply to the angelic sin the three Augustinian basic powers of man: memory, understanding and will. This means – if we take the words of St Ignatius seriously and really understand what he wanted to say and undoubtedly said very imperfectly – not only the application of formal powers to an external object that happens to be there, it means really becoming aware in this triple direction of that basic constituent of our nature which already bears the mark of a created decision. In our memory the recollection of this fall is always present in an unimaginable, but true sense; and an intellectual dynamism steering our own intellectual activity towards this sin exists already as a result of the angels' sin. The same holds for the will.

If we are christians – that is, the redeemed – who are encompassed by grace, then it may be said that this angelic existential in the depths of our existence is not simply removed, but caught up, taken up into a new form and always present. We say: I know from the depth of my existence that sin is possible, because this existence was already sinful in an ultimate source. This possibility can never be taken away from me: from thence, prior to my freedom, I am the one who remembers this possibility. From the depth of my being, made intellectually aware, I am the one who now understands how to use a fine dialectical skill to make something worth-while out of sin; from the depth of my existence, co-determined by the angels, I am from the start the one who perceives already a dynamism, a will to sin (and as one redeemed in Christ, I say "No" to this past of mine and thereby redeem it): a dynamism in which all this endowment of primal sin[1] from the angels is transformed in my memory, understanding and will into these relics, the source of an inner conflict akin to that which arises – as we are accustomed to say expressly with the church – from the concupiscence left by man's original sin.

3. *The sin of our first parents*

We must consider the sin of our first parents (51). Always remember that Adam is not just anybody. Adam lived in the grace of Christ. Adam is somehow the permanent ground of my existence and – no matter how much I am the descendant and not the original – is in the last resort myself. I recognise myself in him, not only because he has the same nature, but as my father. And he is a sinner. He has sinned and that means something for me.

We have to consider Adam's sin: the sin of unbelief,

---

[1] *Ursünde*. "Original sin" is the usual translation, but this might be confused with man's first sin. The author is speaking of the angels' sin at the dawn of creation, prior to all human acts of choice.

the sin against hope, the sin against love, the sin before God, the sin in regard to the fruit of the world, the sin of pride and of weakness in an indissoluble unity. We have to consider the consequences of sin: the one world-history in which sin and the evolution willed by God can no longer be completely taken apart – since sin occurred at the beginning – and in which its lasting consequence is transformed only through the greater grace of Christ. We ought then to conclude that the redemption is not simply the exclusion of the original existential of sin as a constituent of the world, derived from the angels and from Adam; that it means rather coming to terms with this sin and its consequences by incorporating them in a radical, in fact a divine context. This is redemption; but for the most part we don't want to admit it. For we want paradise, the tree of paradise, not the tree of the cross.

Consider this original sinfulness as our situation, the situation of each one of us, as the situation of weakness, in which the permanent power of freedom can be exercised in a wholly remarkable way and which at the same time always finds in this weakness the incentive for itself and its power and the deceitful excuse for its own wickedness. Consider the situation of death as the heritage of original sin. Since in fact sinfulness has been planted into the origin of the world's history and of my history, consider how much sin for that reason has come to be regarded falsely as inevitable in the world. It is at the beginning in such a way as to appear as something that simply cannot be otherwise: that is, it seems to cease for that very reason to exist as sin.

4. *The sin of the redeemed*

The third point to be considered is the sin of the redeemed (53). Here Ignatius presents us with the christian, the redeemed, engraced, sanctified person, who
has tasted the powers of eternal life, who was called in
baptism, has been fed with the body of Christ, favoured
with all heavenly promises. He can sin and even bring
about his eternal damnation in an act which in fact
sums up his whole life and gives it over to sin. This sin
is of course always too the sin of immeasurable risk.
This means that created freedom always seeks of itself
to involve the whole man, to commit him entirely and
to exhaust him in sin; at the same time however it is
always carried into a situation beyond all that could
be anticipated and for that reason, at the moment when
it acts, when it is creative, at that very moment it becomes indissolubly something endured, imposed,
repelling: God's judgment.

This remarkable dualism of our creaturely freedom
is seen in the situation which Ignatius asks us to consider here: there is a sin in which man suddenly perceives that he is at the end, that there can no longer
be any thought of a conversion, that he doesn't want
to be converted at all, cannot want it, that freedom
and necessity, action and suffering, calculation and
incalculability, have merged into a final unity.

Here there comes to light the peculiarity of the sin
of the creature, especially of the intellectual-worldly
creature that we are. This is the situation in which we
are placed. Remember here too (since we are in fact
concerned with the sin of the redeemed) that it is the
sin which can burst out from everything, with which

we can ruin everything, the occasion of which may be all that exists, high or low, sacred or profane, small or great.

5. *Colloquy of mercy*

At the conclusion Ignatius enjoins on us a colloquy of mercy (53). This is not merely a pious, touching end to the meditation, but this conversation under the cross is placed in the final resumé of all that we have been considering: we understand sin only when we understand the cross and the greater mercy of God. We can start something with sin only if we don't want to pluck it from the tree of the knowledge of good and evil, but flee from it to the greater glory of God's life. That is why this colloquy belongs to the heart of this meditation.

It is only by submitting from the very beginning to the absolute revelation of God's grace in the death of the incarnate *Logos* of God that we can understand anything at all about sin. Only when we accept the absolute freedom which God gives us through his grace – that is, through the offer of his own, absolute reality – do we understand what God wants to tell us when he says: You are a sinner, you can be a sinner; this sin remains always as a possibility for you in all the situations of your pilgrimage; this sin is something you will never admit and can confess only when – redeemed and saved by me, God's eternal goodness – you look back, trembling and with gratitude for your redemption, when you see in it the possibility already overtaken by the grace of God, if and as long as you accept this grace in faith and love.

5 OUR OWN SINS

What Ignatius directs us to consider (55–61) is so clear in its simple immediacy that there is not much to be said about it. A few introductory reflections directly concerned with the subject will be set out here: they may be useful for the meditation as Ignatius envisages it.

1. *Demythologising the ascetical life*

For all its religious and theological profundity, this meditation is meant also to be one which takes a sober, realistic view of life. In our spiritual life we are always in danger of using an enormous, complicated equipment of terminology, of stereotyped formulas and concepts, of ascetic and moral motives, which distract us from taking a cool look at reality. We talk so much about virtues and sins and all the rest and at the same time we have from the very beginning a definite idea of what these things are, of what they look like, so that we perceive only with difficulty their real meaning.

Before we can consider sin in our life, we ought to make a meditation on our life unemotionally and realistically, and at the same time avoid giving it any moral stamp from the very beginning, so that we can come face to face with our reality.

Don't let us ask: Am I humble or arrogant? Do I love God or not? Am I someone who is ready to sacrifice all for the love of Christ or am I not? But let us ask: What am I really making of my life? What am I doing? What kind of a person emerges when I am described for once in the matter of fact terminology of an unbeliever, of a psychologist, of someone who can test my reactions?

Let us look at the people around us, not to judge or condemn them, but in order in this way to produce more easily a technique for self-criticism. Don't we find there – whether among priests or laity – many people of whom we are bound to admit that they certainly want to obey God's commandments and do on the whole obey them and yet we have the impression that a great deal in their lives is terribly wrong. It is no use saying therefore that there is no question at all here of sin, but only of dispositions, peculiarities, of incapacity in one respect or another, that all this is prior to any moral reaction and judgement. This person is in fact like this: he does not get away from himself; perhaps he does not realise at all how out of touch he is, how he under-estimates or over-estimates himself. He does not grasp the fact that he is seeking his effects in a field where they cannot be achieved; he does not notice that he is taking things very easily; he does not feel that there is any moral problem about settling down in comfort, leading a mediocre life, about what a modern psychologist would make of his thousand substitutes for action – certainly morally unquestionable – in which he comes to terms in his solitude with his failure in a scarcely commendable, evil way.

We have only indicated a few of the many things that happen in this way. That is – once again – the life of a particular individual, seen from a human and realistic standpoint, in the light of his mastery of life, and even (we say this quite soberly and seriously) in

the light of his success in life, leaves a very great deal
to be desired; and yet the person concerned thinks that
his moral status is perfectly in order.

Of course it is clear that such a realistic meditation,
coming to grips with life, looking to a person's success,
his inward composure, his joy in life, his contact with
other people – in a word, to the way he masters life on
this earth – and a meditation asking how such a person
stands with God cannot really be made to coincide. It
is even obvious that we would be greatly mistaken in
attempting to consider the two ways simply as two
different ways of expressing one and the same absolutely identical reality. To do so would not only be in-
correct, but it would mean also that we were not
bringing a genuine, radically christian mentality to
our understanding of life. In other words: there are
obviously human inadequacies, twisted outlooks,
meannesses, blindnesses, abnormal reactions in regard
to coping with life, which really have nothing to do
with what a person is morally, in God's judgment.

In the normal, average, religious life, however, these
two ways of meditation lie too far apart. Theoretically
also they are too far apart. For it does in fact remain
true in terms of dogmatic and moral theology, and of
philosophy, that what is right, pertinent, in accordance
with human nature, whatever consists in harmony
with reality and is therefore also in harmony with God,
that this too is moral. From a dogmatic standpoint, it
remains absolutely correct that those objective twists
of character, the stupid opinions, bad habits, limitations of talent, which are perhaps beyond the control
of human freedom, are also in fact the very thing that
ought not to be.

If I see that someone is fundamentally lazy, does not exploit his talents, fails to set about his tasks as forcefully, radically and energetically as another person applies himself to his secular calling in order to achieve something and to earn a living, I don't solve the problem by saying: The poor fellow doesn't understand his situation, he doesn't know about it, he means well, somewhere at least he is in touch with reality, but he is objectively blind to the possibilities and opportunities in his life. This does in fact raise the question whether this blindness in regard to life's real opportunities is inculpable. The person concerned may claim to have a good conscience, but perhaps it is only apparently good: he has perhaps heaped up on his innermost personal conviction so much rubbish by way of pretexts, surrenders in his life, of cowardice and cheap excuses, that he now thinks everything is in order.

Before saying that we are sinners, we would have to examine our lives calmly in the light of standards that are applied today. The weakness of touch, the introversion, the unease, the traumata, which we fail to transcend: these and a thousand other aspects would first have had to be observed in an appropriate consideration of our own person before we could ask: What have these to do with sin? Only then could we ask: At what points do we find the basically sinful roots of our condition which we have just examined so realistically?

The same holds for the danger of wrecking our life. If we say *a priori* that we are human and capable of sin, then again there is a danger of overlooking the real sins. Let us raise now the moral question: Where, at what point, through what causes, can my life with its tasks, with its possibilities, break down? (It is all the same whether anything or nothing could be done about it – this is another problem.) We would first have to discover prior to any moral judgment where the danger of such a breakdown lies. Does it arise from health, from my stupidity, from an innate difficulty in measuring up to what I ought to achieve? Are there any other things that could ruin my life, moral or immoral, or having nothing to do with morality? Am I in danger of a spectacular catastrophe?

The danger of a spectacular breakdown does exist. But at least equally serious is the danger that our whole life will slowly but surely fade into oblivion: the danger of mediocrity, of no longer really believing in a personal achievement, of giving up everything.

There is of course one capitulation that is imposed on everyone: we grow old, sick, tired, face the approach of death. There is also real breakdown, a hopeless situation, which is the proper achievement of our lives, perhaps imposed on us and required of us by God. Why should this not be the case? Someone could be called to a position in the church for which he was not really suited, where even with the best will and with heroic efforts, from a purely human, intramundane standpoint, he cannot make much of his situation.

Such things do happen and we are right, but perhaps over hasty, to speak of them as our share in the cross of Christ. Before we think of these things, maintaining our sober, realistic view of life, we might ask: Before we pass any moral judgment, where is the danger of failing in regard to our positive, genuine, possible, attainable task in life? Such a failure must not be described at once as a sin. The question is not so much whether it is a sin or not, but how this sort of thing can be avoided.

Not much is gained merely by stating the moral requirement in regard to this task: Do this.

Let us be honest. We preach and listen to others preaching too many moral imperatives and axioms and we far too rarely present ourselves and others with the question: How do I set about fulfilling what is required of me and how do I avoid what has to be avoided? It is an old-fashioned, but absurd view that a person knows without more ado how he has to set about doing something and that the only problem is whether he wills to do so or not.

Of course, each man in his original, spiritual, personal freedom is also faced with decisions whether he will or not: will you respect this norm of God or not? Will you risk the leap or will you nervously stick to your present position and refuse to accept this task? But when my confessor tells me to fight against distractions at meditation, he has not told me how to set about it.

An example of this kind shows that the way in which in the concrete we have to satisfy a moral demand that life imposes is a question to itself and very much a question of content, and it must be distinguished from the question of what moral requirements are imposed on me. This "how" or "in what way" has no direct connection with strenuous moral effort or anything of that kind, but relates to a practical way – one might say, a skill – and to a rational, practical knowledge of how something must be done.

It is useless to advise someone who is out of touch to interest himself in his fellow-men, to have a heart full of love for all. It is of little use to tell someone who is nervous to be bold and take a risk. What is required is

57

a calm consideration of the situation in a perspective, in categories and terms, which to a certain extent ascetically demythologise one's life and then really permit things to be seen as they are. Then you may ask: "How do I come to terms with these things?"

1. *Sin, venial sin, and fundamental decision*

When we have ascetically demythologised our life, we can ask the further question: Where are our sins to be found? Or, more cautiously: Where are the dangers of sin lurking? Then we can and must say: Sin, in the theological sense, is a reality in my life. It is a fact, it is a permanent possibility, it is always a danger, it is always something which in the last resort I cannot judge or measure, in face of which I always flee to God's mercy. Sin is a reality in my life, for "if we say that we have no sin, we deceive ourselves" (1 Jn 1:8). And the Council of Trent teaches (DS 1573) that it is false to say that "without a special privilege from God, it is possible to avoid all sins, even venial, for a whole life-time." But when we assert that it is not possible to avoid all venial sins in the course of a whole lifetime, aren't we turning this terrible fact into something trivial and dangerously simple by claiming that it is a question merely of venial sins, of surreptitious sins?

Even assuming that it is a question only of venial sins, we don't want to conceal the fact that venial sin too can sometimes be a dreadful handicap to our apostolate, perhaps more so than a grave sin. Indolence, love of comfort, uncharitableness, arrogance – in a word, the sort of thing that gets on the nerves of laypeople when they see it in clerics – are often only venial sins, but how damaging they are to aid for souls, to our apostolate, to the reputation of the church. But in connection with the statement that not all venial sins can be avoided throughout a whole lifetime, there is another fact to which we should pay more attention.

Are we so sure that manifestations of the basis of our human existence, rightly or at least with probability described as venial sins, do not emerge from a primal source of our spiritual personality that is itself in a state of grave sin? There is a "global commitment", there is a basic, human decision which remains anonymous, which cannot be grasped concretely in its material detail, cannot be judged and arrested, and yet nevertheless exists. When we consider our venial sins, we must therefore ask ourselves if they are really so harmless in this respect. Is the proposition that all men, without special aid from God, commit venial sins likewise innocuous? There is a final infidelity, a final cowardice, a final refusal to give ourselves to God, a final want of love, a final egoism, which render it completely unnecessary to admit to ourselves that final rejection of God which comes from the depth of our soul: we can in fact refuse to see that our trivial faults and imperfections are a cover for a final basic attitude which is truly mortal sin.

Are there not people of whom we are inclined to say that they have in fact committed some grave sin and perhaps not yet got out of it, but in the last resort are loving, selfless, inwardly looking to God, more than some others who nervously avoid introducing any kind of disorder into the tidy pattern of their lives? One of those beatified as martyrs at the time of the Boxer rebellion had been a hopeless opium addict and always said that his only chance lay in martyrdom, although in other respects he was a devout christian. His parish priest – rightly, it might seem – refused absolution for years. Yet, if this man longed for martyrdom, really knew and admitted before God how miserable and wretched he was and asked God to free him from his self-imposed imprisonment, may we not ask if, even before his martyrdom, his life was not really rooted and founded in the love of God – more perhaps than that of the parish priest who rightly refused absolution?

If we say then in theological terms that sin is a reality and always an immediate possibility in our lives, we should not make light of this proposition. The more or less indefinable character of venial sin, which we really commit (as christians we cannot deny this), does in fact make our situation endurable only if we get away from ourselves and flee to God alone, loving and trusting in his mercy. Understood in this way, anyone can make a meditation on his own sins, even if he is quite sure from the standpoint of moral theology – that is, as far as his duty of confession is concerned – that he plainly and clearly has not committed any grave sin. The person is not for that reason justified before God. For even if he were justified, he has always to remember that this is due to the more radical salvation through grace on God's side and not to his own merits.

3. Sin as reality encompassed by God's grace

If however our theological consideration of sin leads (according to Ignatius) to the conclusion that sin is a reality in my past, in my present, and a radically menacing possibility in my future, then we may and must also conclude that it is reality encompassed by

God's grace. God's grace, God's love, God's will to salvation in Jesus Christ is really greater than our sin. We can never say that we are certainly justified, predestined to eternal life. As true christians therefore, who have understood what Christ, the incarnation, the cross and redemption, really mean, we may not preach christianity as a commandment of God and as offering a possibility on which we decide only in an ultimate sovereignty which is not encompassed by God. We would then have to preach to christians that God has given certain commandments and, in what we call grace, the possibility of keeping these commandments.

This is important and right and must always be preached. But the question remains whether this way of preaching christianity is adequate, whether we cannot ourselves make more of it. The answer must be that we can. I cannot of course claim to be certainly predestined to eternal life; but I must to some extent open the ears of faith and the heart of hope, not in order to produce a theoretical proposition about my predestination and God's salvific will, but to listen to God's word telling me: I love you in a way which in fact includes your freedom, and by loving you (we call this efficacious grace), I give you what you have to do.

Of course we cannot indulge in theories about this, we cannot turn it into a theoretical proposition about "the restoration of all things". It must never become a weapon against God, an excuse for taking things easily, a dispensation for ourselves. But if we strive with all that we have and are to get away from ourselves and run to God, if and in as much as we do this, in the dimension of christian hope, in spite of the sins which are real enough in our life, we have the right to accept from God the assurance: I love you, you who are a sinner, and my grace is more powerful, more loving, and embraces all that you are, even your sin.

In the light of all this, the christian's meditation is a meditation on where he comes from, not on where he is going; it is a meditation on what he would be of himself and not a meditation on what he is by the grace of God. Such a meditation on sin therefore, if it is truly christian – that is, if it sees the human, true, responsible freedom, which a man cannot throw on to anyone else, as nevertheless encompassed, sustained, redeemed by the grace of God – is a meditation on our own sin which is an expression of the gratitude of redeemed love, which from this source has the courage to transcend its own limitations, to sacrifice what it cannot sacrifice by its own strength, to set about doing what it could not do from its own resources. Think of Augustine, who knew what he had to do and thought he could find no strength in himself. He looked – so to speak – into the empty jar of his own finiteness and asked how he could accomplish what he ought to do.

Whenever it is a question of real decisions against sin and for God, it is impossible to feel and enjoy first of all the capacity for these things and then to act accordingly. Nevertheless, we can always act in virtue of our powerlessness, jump while absolutely dreading the leap, because God is with us, because – without our being able to observe and as it were enjoy it in advance – our impotence, our weakness, and our cowardice, are always surpassed by God's power and mercy, by his grace: grace which frees us for action and is not merely the means as a sort of autonomous – and what Augustine might call emancipated – freedom. Understood in this way, Molinism would not be Molinism, but theological nonsense and an appalling, existentially false attitude for a christian. We are those who, in the gratitude of redeemed love, find the courage to say "Yes" to God and his demand.

4. *Triple colloquy*

In the light of all this, the triple colloquy (63), which Ignatius enjoins on us, is obvious: to Mary, pure, sinless, who was this and was what she was only by grace, by the purest grace; the sinless one, in the flesh of sin, in our adamitic situation, in the darkness of the world, was involved in the risk which is ours also. For that reason, being the one who is absolutely redeemed, she is much closer to us than anyone who would have to say: I too am a sinner.

We should say the *Anima Christi* before Christ, the Son of the Father, the incarnate one, the redeemer, before him who died our death in the flesh of sin.

We should say the "Our Father" to "the Father of mercies and God of all comfort" (2 Cor. 1:3), to the Father who is not only the incomprehensible mystery in himself, but also alone the ultimate mystery of our existence. We are the mystery and he knows it. To a certain extent, as mystery withdrawn from itself (however much we know who we are, but without being able to say this to ourselves), we can flee to him who shelters this mystery in himself, knows it, sustains it, created it and engraces it, wills to take it into himself and his eternal life. The abyss of fearful possibility that we are flees into the abyss which we call God and of whom we say, when we do this: he is eternal love, the one whom we can really call "Father".

6 THE KINGDOM OF CHRIST

In the second week of the *Exercises* Ignatius wants the retreatant to come to a choice. This is a choice of means, not of the end. At the point where they are to be selected, from the first, in themselves and objectively, these means are all morally positive or at least indifferent. It is a question of a decision, not between good and evil, but between different means, all of which can serve objectively for the attainment of one and the same goal. It is obviously not easy to say which among the means presented to our choice is the better. These meditations, especially this on the kingdom of Christ, are put forward by Ignatius in order to create the necessary presuppositions for this act of choice which is the real and decisive element in the *Exercises*. He wants to use this meditation to prepare us for the right attitude in our choice, so that we are not deaf to the call of the Lord in whatever form it may come.

It is another question, however, how far we can and should now make a retreat leading to an effective choice. We can proceed only in the direction of the way chosen once and for all. But there are constantly occasions in our life when we are faced with a choice of greater or lesser moment and in the retreat it should be possible at least to allow for the fact that these situations do occur in which and in regard to which we have to make a choice. To this extent we can always pray for the right attitude to our choice, which always precedes the choice itself.

Since we are always in danger of reducing what we have rightly chosen into something objectivistic, institutionalistic, commonplace; since with the right choice of means the right disposition, which once led to the choice of these means, is not guaranteed; and since in fact what is important is the ultimate disposition from which this choice of concrete living conditions sprang, we can constantly make this meditation which brings out what is most important and culminates in the "oblation of greater worth and moment" (97).

As Ignatius envisages it in the *Exercises*, a disposition should take concrete form in the corporality of a particular way of life; it is the other way round with us who are priests, for here the concrete form of life must be constantly filled out and in the light of this the spirit of the absolute imitation of Christ which it implies must be roused. The point of this meditation is preparedness for the right attitude of choice.

1. *Jesus Christ is Lord*

First of all, Ignatius sets our Lord Jesus Christ before our eyes. There is no human life that is great and meaningful unless it is risked in the service of a greater cause. When a person is self-seeking, when he makes himself the centre of his life, that life becomes empty and meaningless. The greater cause, however, to which a man must give himself up if his life is to be meaningful, is not really a greater cause, but a greater person.

The great person, the living person, who can call on all life's forces, who can rightly lay claim to all powers, whom we can personally love, is ultimately the absolute person of God. We christians know however that this absolute person, to whom we unreservedly abandon our whole life and in whose service we place ourselves completely, is not the infinitely distant God, but the God who is close, who is flesh, who is where we are, who is like us, who as the absolute mystery is at the same time of one nature with us, just as the *Logos* is also of one nature with the Father. This incarnate God, in the *Exercises*, is the one who is calling to us, calling us away from ourselves, whom to serve is reward enough.

This royal Lord, existing here and now in our historicity and nevertheless the absolute God, is one who is coming, whose history still continues in the history of his brothers and sisters, of the humanity of which he is a member, in the history of his church and his world. The royal Lord, who can radically lay claim to our life, absolutely and in all situations, as no one else could, is that one who nevertheless has a history: this call coming from him to us really belongs to him, it is a piece of his own life, so that he calls us into his own destiny, since he is himself still the one who is coming. Christ living, still active, his destiny not yet entirely achieved, although the absolutely decisive thing in his life has already occurred through his death and resurrection: this Christ, who is in the midst of history (this remains true even after the ascension and glorification of the Lord) and shares with us its torment and tasks, this Christ calls us to be with him.

It would be possible to outline a kind of aprioristic christology in the light of the fact that an absolute claim is made on man by the greater cause, the greater person, who is still coming and calls us in the midst of our history. It is in fact a good thing to look at the question a little from this aspect. At the same time however (and this is the decisive point) we know that this royal Lord has his own personal name: with his own life in the midst of the history of our world, he lays claim and wants to lay claim to us; we seek him in order to get started at all; we need him when we who serve have to give up, we need him if we don't want to be stifled within our own narrow lives. This one who thus calls and can lay claim to us is Jesus of Nazareth. This is the tremendous and, at the same time, obvious truth of our christian faith.

We know that there is one to whom we must bring our life, our strength, the meaning of our existence; we know that we are those who by our very nature must ask: "Are you he who is to come?" (Mt 11:3) Are you taking me away from myself? Are you the one whom to serve is really its own reward? If we know all this, we know at the same time that we have found him: Jesus of Nazareth. He is the one who is calling, the one on whom we have to meditate here.

2. *The call to imitate Christ*

In accordance with the sequence of the *Exercises*, we now have to consider Jesus' invitation to us. Jesus first of all summons men to follow him. To a life as personal love for him, to knowing and willing that his life should be extended to us as the entelechy of our life. His Spirit (in the theological sense of the word) who shaped this life of his, should encroach on us. We should follow him as master, as Lord, as the beloved, as the one who is faithfully imitated, as him whose life, destiny, mission and death we have to share.

3. *Imitation in a life of effort*

The second thing to which this invitation of the royal

Lord draws our attention is that this personally loving, faithful, absolute imitation is a life of effort. We see in this imitation that the christian life consists in a veritable fight for life. This too is not simple and obvious: that the christian life is effort, is bitter, is difficult – difficult for me, so difficult that it seems improbable, almost too much to ask. There is much that is difficult which one person may find easy; there are things which perhaps in themselves are easy, banal, and yet difficult for me. To explain the christian life as the imitation of Christ does not make this imitation any easier. It is true that our Lord says that his yoke is easy and his burden light (Mt 11:30); but even if we know that we are imitating Christ, our life as christians in that form is toilsome, arduous, narrow, wretched, it means death and pain, misery, the courage always to continue the fight. This is the meaning of our Lord's command, that those who follow him must have the same food and the same drink that he has, must labour as he does during the day and watch during the night, and so on (93).

4. Obedient acceptance of God's decree

This struggle and hardship of christian life is of course part of the hardship, the narrowness, the death-trend of human life generally. Christ's summons to us here, then, is to what is largely inescapable in human life and lies also as a burden on pagans who have not heard the call to the imitation of Christ. This summons encourages us to accept voluntarily and without protest what constitutes the destiny, the burden, the struggle and the agony of every life and is often endured better by those possessed of a grace they cannot name and who do not know that their life is an imitation of the cross of Christ. They endure all this better than we do for all our talk about imitating Christ and about generosity: we often present a lamentable appearance in the most ordinary affairs of life while the pagans can accept sickness and death often with silent resignation, can bear the uselessness of their calling, stick to their position, and often give up their comfort more easily than we do who claim to be followers of the crucified Christ. Christ's summons to imitate him, so far as it is difficult, is a summons first of all and originally to a loving, obedient, freely chosen acceptance of God's plan, in which we are involved anyway.

Let us consider further how man's "Yes" takes concrete shape, "consider that all who have the use of judgment and reason will offer their whole selves for labour" (96). What is meant here first of all is the obedience which readily submits to God's plan as it is revealed in the crucified life of Jesus. These labours are essentially those which fill every life: endurance to the end of human life in its narrowness, poverty, uselessness, its assignment to death.

Only stupid people could think that life is not like this, for even happiness still lies over an abyss of misery and death. When a man offers himself then with judgment and reason to share those labours of Christ which are in fact the labour, the burden, the futility of mankind generally, he is offering his assent to what has been decreed, his freedom to something suffered, his acceptance of the unsought burden, and he is therefore first of all acknowledging the abysmal character of our existence and voluntarily making the leap towards the unassailable.

5. *The voluntary step towards the cross*

We come to the last point (97, 98): the voluntary advance to what is ultimately God's decree even if we did not voluntarily accept it. These "oblations" essentially take voluntarily that short step towards God's plan which we are not yet bound to take. What we offer Christ here is a voluntary step towards him who, with the inescapable human lot as Son of Man, comes in any case to us and disposes of us.

What is new in the "more" and "acting against" is the going forward. Every man is someone crucified; when he accepts this condition, he is a christian; and what Ignatius still wants beyond this as "more" and "acting against" means no more than going forward a very little towards this crucified life that comes upon us in any case, so that now the assent to what is decreed and the deed in absolute endurance are really effected.

Whence do I know that I shall one day accept with faith death in its cruelty, in its absolute impotence and emptiness, as the death of Christ? Whence do I know that I shall accept my human life, enduring it to the end, not in imitation of Adam, but in imitation of Christ? I shall really know only when I find the courage purely from the grace of God to go a little way towards him and already to accept a little of the cross of Christ while I could still avoid it. Considered in this way, the religious life does not seek to overtake and surpass the christian life under the cross and in imitation of Christ, but seeks only one thing: to do everything to secure the success of this christian life and that is why these "offers of greater worth and moment" are made. This is the meaning of the "more" and "acting against". Read the prayer of oblation (98), and ask yourself whether you have the courage to say these words sincerely to God and his Christ. Don't be thinking from the first that this is already realised in your life. When you read about "bearing all insults and reproaches, and all poverty, and so on", apply that to the situation of your own life and ask yourself: Where do I go voluntarily, even though with fear and trembling, overcoming my own cowardice, at some point towards the cross of Christ? Where have I the courage at least to pray for these sentiments? Or am I someone who has taken on the life of a priest indeed, but finds little there that is more burdensome than the life of other people? We have not suffered more hunger, stupid superiors have not heaped on us more insults and reproaches than a clerk has to suffer and put up with from his chief, or a wife from her husband. Let us ask God for the grace to understand a little of what is involved here and to venture at least to pray for a little of it.

I know a German philosopher, a politician, who is not a christian. During the Nazi period he was imprisoned and could expect to be killed. This man knew the prayer of Pius x: "I accept even now any kind of death from your hand . . ." Although he was an avowed non-christian, he asked himself in prison: If I say this, will God take me at my word? And yet he tried to say it. He escaped death.[1] Nevertheless, that was an absolutely decisive moment for him, to say once to God: If this is the end, if I am now going to be hanged, then it is right, it shall be so. I accept what comes upon me as the great deed from within, in

[1] F. Hielscher, *Fünfzig Jahre unter Deutschen*, Hamburg, 1954, p 411.

which I truly realise (for once in a christian sense) that you, the eternal, living God in Christ and his destiny are worth more to me than I am to myself, than my life, than all that I might wish for myself of happiness, of self-assertion.

We should read this text of the *Exercises*, this prayer (98), almost with a kind of horror. If we say this prayer sincerely, God can take us too at our word and dispose of our life, so that we can say: Lead me, I no longer know which way to turn; give me your grace to remain to the end truly imitating the crucified Lord.

7 THE INCARNATION

In the course of the *Exercises* there now follows the meditation on the incarnation (101–109). This provides an opportunity to consider both the theological principles and the historical facts as narrated in the gospels.

1. *The christocentrism of all reality*

We must first work out some abstract ideas on the christocentrism of all reality. Today particularly it would be apologetically prejudicial to try to present the incarnation of the eternal word merely as a secondary solution which God subsequently takes up in order to overcome man's sin. If the incarnation is considered merely as one factor within the whole course of history, the question at once arises whether the incarnation has decisively altered the course of the history of sinful mankind.

We shall allow for this objection by starting out from the more fundamental consideration, recognising the decision of the eternal God for the incarnation as the basic intention of God in his creation. Theologically speaking, we certainly have the right and the opportunity – if not even the duty – to see the grace of the angels and likewise the grace of Adam in paradise as the grace of Christ. We can then understand nature, the present world, secular realities, the facts of world-history, as what God himself presupposes as the condition making possible his self-utterance in the non-divine and created world.

73

We can see "nature" as what must be in order that the real truth may be understood: that God himself may come out from himself as absolute *agape* and express himself in what is not God. Thus the decision of the eternal God to impart himself to the non-divine is God's absolutely first and comprehensive decision. It is the basic, all-inclusive decision, which did not have to be changed because of man's sin but acquired thereby a particular tone, in so far as this sin as rebellion of the free creature (angels and men) against God remains in fact outstripped and encompassed by God's greater decision to make his own self-utterance in the non-divine. Since in fact it is not and cannot be removed by sin, this decision of God for self-utterance is therefore by that very fact also a redemptive decision in regard to this finite reality, in as much as the latter, precisely in virtue of its own nature, and in virtue of the peculiarity of its freedom, is capable of being redeemed: this is indeed the case with man, for in him the time for freedom still continues.

Thus we are in a position to see the fundamental mysteries of christianity – Trinity, incarnation, grace and glory – as one comprehensive mystery. There is therefore really only one basic mystery: that the absolute God in the unrelatedness and glory of his own life founded in himself, who is therefore dependent on nothing other than himself, goes out as himself into the non-divine, utters himself, imparts himself.

This self-communication comes to be in an incarnation and grace, with these two mysteries being necessarily connected, since we can and must accept the fact that this one and divine decision to go out of himself in radical self-communication is free. But when this free decision of God occurs, it comes about necessarily in an incarnation and therefore necessarily in humanity – the humanity within which this self-utterance of God occurs – and indeed as engraced humanity – that is to say, incarnation and divinisation of all reality in view of the free creature are necessarily connected. This one incarnatory-engracing, transfiguring, divinising, self-communication of God to the world, which is created in this decision for his own utterance, reveals precisely what we call the mystery of the Trinity: from this standpoint too the redemptive-historical ("economic") Trinity and the inner, immanent Trinity are intrinsically one; both are the same thing and the true reality of the Trinity is revealed in this self-communication and not only in theoretical propositions.

It is within this framework that the incarnation must properly be seen if it is to be understood. Then it is indeed something that happens in a moment of time, but also that which as inner entelechy sustains from the very beginning the totality of the world, of creation and its history. The whole world is planned from the very beginning in the light of this, the whole world in its history aims at this. In this incarnation the world is brought together in a unity; and in this incarnation its eternal, final destiny, as redeemed, as positive, is not only promised, but essentially already accomplished.

In the light of all this, creation as *creatio rei ex nihilo sui et subiecti* is to be understood once again as an element in the greater action of God, in his self-utterance. Because and in so far as he can utter himself and this possibility of the freedom of his *agape* is part of that which is most essential in his nature, he can be creator; because in fact he willed this free self-utterance

75

of his – so to speak – as the lavishing of himself, he also actually willed this creation as such. He is creator in as much as and because he willed to be the giver of grace. He wanted to be grace-giving because he wanted to be self-communicating. He was able and wanted to be this, because the absolute, incomprehensible mystery is also the mystery of God's *agape*.

2. *The meaning of the incarnation*

When we see the incarnation in this light, we must grasp the fact that in the incarnation God – in Augustine's words – creates by assuming (*assumendo creat*). The incarnation – and this is of fundamental importance for our ascetic and religious life – properly speaking is not the assumption of anything into the person of God, but the humanity of the *Logos* comes to be precisely in and through the fact that God wills to utter himself. When the eternal *Logos* of the Father communicates and wants to communicate himself to the non-divine, there comes to be precisely what we call his humanity. This means then that his humanity is not some kind of a livery, an instrument which God uses as a sign, but which in itself would express nothing at all about him: the humanity of Christ is the real self-utterance of the *Logos*, as assumed of course, as that which is hypostatically united with the *Logos*, but for that very reason as itself.

This humanity is not the mask of a God who then again remains absolutely concealed beneath the outward clothing; it is not something from which, properly speaking, nothing can be known about him who assumed humanity, so that this humanity would become a self-revelation, a *parousia* of God and of the

Logos, only when God begins to act with the humanity, to make in it some kind of important statements or to do particularly striking things, to work miracles and the like. No: this humanity itself as such is the truthful, real self-utterance of this *Logos*, in such a way of course that this self-utterance can never exhaustively express the divine *Logos*. He – the *Logos* – remains of course in this self-utterance the unfathomable mystery. But precisely as such it is present, it is grasped, it has its *parousia* in this humanity and is now really a presence of this absolute mystery that we call God and is available to us through the fact that God is man.

In the light of this, man in general must be understood up to a point as God's wording, through which and by means of which he can express himself, and the humanity of Christ as the real utterance of God. If man is absolute openness to God, if he is the one who is radically capable of receiving and the one who knows of this absolute receptive openness, if he is the one who knows and understands that his origin is absolutely directly from God, then – whether he knows it or not – he understands himself already as image of the *Logos*, who is the utterance of the Father, absolute receptivity for the Father.

This image of the *Logos* that man is essentially and from the first now becomes also the self-utterance of the *Logos*, so that the God-man is the image of the eternal image of the Father in one, the image that from eternity as Word of the Father finds expression within the dimension of the created world. This God-man in his incomparable unity of divinity and humanity is really the sole point at which we can understand, accept and live fundamentally the relation of God to

77

what is not God and in which we can be saved.

3. *Incarnation and imitation*

From this outline you can see that man's opportunity and obligation of imitating Christ, established by the incarnation, is not primarily and essentially an imitation of the particular moral virtues and acts of the God-man, but first and last an imitation in the acceptance of human existence. Man as person is precisely the one who has to deal with his own nature, who in his being present to himself, his *reditio completa ad seipsum* (Aquinas), and in his freedom actively disposes not of just anything, but of himself: in both, man is that one who is placed before himself and asked how he will come to terms with himself.

In the light of this transcendence and this freedom and this dependence on the absolute God, it is by no means obvious that this man is in harmony with himself. He can protest – so to speak – against this preexistent reality, he can feel that he is "condemned to freedom", he can rebel against this constriction which is imposed in him, which befalls him and which he experiences, which he knows but can never overcome. In other words: he really has a free relationship to his own life which bears the character of a decision.

All sanctity, all sin can be regarded in the last resort as acceptance or rejection by man of this, his own human existence. Every sin is really a "No" to this human nature and to the control it possesses in advance over man's freedom, human life and human nature being always understood of course as the actual nature, nature with its supernatural vocation through participation in the life of God. In the light of this, imitation of Christ then means first and last the acceptance of our own human existence with its goal: the achievement in our turn of that assumption of human nature which the eternal *Logos* himself achieved.

To be in harmony with what now in fact belongs to this nature, with its corporality, its sexuality, its constriction, its death-trend, with its pain, its shared existence with others, its earthly origin, with its incorporation into the history of nature and the rest of mankind, its association too with the principalities and authorities which we call angels: all this is properly speaking the task that life puts before us. All that we call moral, ethical, is nothing other than the ought-character of this objective confrontedness with oneself and one's existence. When this existence is accepted, the ought-character of this existence is then *ipso facto* fulfilled and all this holds (whether we know it or not) in the concrete, thoroughly christocentric order of reality; all this is an achievement of the assumption of humanity, of human existence, by the eternal *Logos* who himself accepts his image in it or – better – projects himself as the image of the Father into the non-divine, thereby expressing the human reality, so that in the assumption of human existence by Christ and the Father we are ourselves assumed.

This cannot be understood of course as an assumption of any kind of abstract human nature, of something that could be reduced to a purely formal structure – as, for instance, "rational animal". What is always meant is actual human existence: that which is projected by the Father in the *Logos*, which is expressed by the *Logos* himself in his incarnation, which is conceived and willed from the first as sharing the world of the incarnate *Logos*. This human nature we always accept, not as something we have understood, but as something imposed on us as the enigma of our own existence. Hence no one succeeds in getting away from this christocentrism of human life. Every man must thus confirm his freedom in the acceptance or rejection of this human existence of his and – up to a point – is inescapably really bound to do this.

Through christian revelation we know more of this ontological depth of human life, but every man has to deal with this life as it is, known reflexively or as something not understood, with which he is necessarily faced. Whether he knows it or not, everyone accepts Christ with the free acceptance of his existence or rejects in protest the Christ imposed on him.

In regard to this imitation of Christ, it must be remembered that this humanity as it exists in Christ, in the actual shape of that life's destiny, is also the existential of our own life. We are not simply projected and sustained by the *Logos* who has assumed an abstract human nature, but by the *Logos* who willed and accomplished this human life in fact as his revelation and self-utterance in the finite world. That is why everything concrete about this human life tells us what is really intended with us.

The Christ-conformation of existence is not merely the result of the abstract assumption of human nature by the *Logos*, but comes about through the actual shape of existence. That is why we meditate on the life of Christ, why we say we will imitate our Lord in his poverty, why we say that our life is a participation in the death and in the cross of Christ. All these things have a certain contingency in the life of Jesus; they did not need to be so, they are again concrete expressions of a free attitude of the *Logos*, who wanted to reveal himself just in this way. But it is just this actual shape of the life of Jesus which then becomes the law of our life, whether we can draw this conclusion in a theoretical, abstract moral philosophy or moral theology, or not. In regard to this life we cannot ask Jesus why he did this or that; at any rate, we cannot ask about everything, down to the last detail.

The life of Jesus as form of our life cannot be regarded merely as an alternative: either to reject it, to consider it as invalid for us, or to prove it to be appropriate in actuality by the standards of an abstract, fundamentally essentialist philosophy of man and what he ought to do. The Lord is the ultimate standard; there is none higher than he, since the ultimate standard of necessity is revealed to us just in this actual person. For it is just here that the *Logos* became man and not simply any man, but this man, so that we cannot really accept a division in the life of Jesus between what is important for us and what can be left aside, however true it may be that the structure of this life bears within itself and thus also creates for us variations of significance and of necessity. All this remains a factor of this unique historical norm, and the imitation of Christ can be measured by no other standard than Jesus himself and his life.

4. *Persons involved in the incarnation*

After these more or less theoretical reflections, we can turn to the points which Ignatius puts before us in the meditation on the incarnation (106–108). We shall look at the persons concerned, the world in its diversity, in its unity, in its unsurmountable human weakness, in its desperation.

For this world of ours the God-man is still the one who is to come and still permanently represents the omega point for this whole history. The increasingly rapid evolution of the present time does not pass Christ by, nor does it catch up with him. For the absolute unity of the infinite God with the intellectual creature, which exists in Christ, in which the world becomes aware of itself, is unsurpassable for all evolution whether chronologically prior to it or coming after it. All unification of the world and mankind is still only an approximation to what God himself as unity, as confirmation of the world, has already created in Jesus Christ. The world still continues to approach God, because God has already become absolutely close to it in Jesus Christ.

Ignatius leads us to meditate not only on the world into which the eternal *Logos* is born, but also on God, the redeeming Father, the Son and the Spirit. The Father, the nameless, unoriginated origin of all reality who, when he utters himself, necessarily speaks in the Son and not otherwise; and when he utters himself and thus imparts himself to the world – and indeed the whole world – gives himself in the Spirit of the Father and the Son. So it is and not otherwise, so that of course, seen from this standpoint, the incarnation is really a work of the triune God, not merely because the hypostatic union is brought about effectively by the one God as causal principle, but because in the hypostatic union the Trinity is necessarily revealed in its own proper reality and made present in the world. The utterance of the Father in the world is the eternal, intra-divine *Logos* as incarnate and thus the world is in fact already engraced by God in the sense that it is filled and engraced by God's holy Spirit; and what is thus present in the world in the self-communicating reality of God is the Trinity in God himself.

Among the persons to be considered is also the blessed virgin. She, the virgin – that is, the one who is still unreservedly at God's disposal, holy and sinless – she is the handmaid of the Lord who, by this fact, fulfils her whole destiny, has her whole dignity, and is the one who receives the word of God in mind and body as one: this is because, where pure, sinless creation exists and reaches its peak, conception in mind and body becomes one, since in fact mind and body together in absolute unity constitute man. And she is the one who shares one destiny with her child, who conceives this child as the redeemer of the world. Although he is born of Mary, in whom the *Logos* himself in his redemptive coming into the world creates the fully redeemed presupposition of his coming, the virgin is also one who belongs to this world of flesh, of sin, of death and therefore conceives the *Logos* as the man of the cross, receiving in her destiny that of her child too.

5. *The event of the incarnation*

In addition to the persons, we are to consider the event. "The Word became flesh," says John (1:14): the Word then has received the body of sin, is under the necessity of the law, of death, poverty, emptiness, grief, servitude and tears. In all this the Word of God appears. "In this" is perhaps not really the exact expression. We should perhaps say: "At this point".

This is the tremendous paradox of christianity: the unredeemed is assumed and redeemed. For so it is. We are to be redeemed from death and therefore death was assumed as the fate of the *Logos* himself. We were to be redeemed from our existential poverty, emptiness and desperation, and therefore he became poor for our sakes (Phil 3:8–9), therefore he endured to the end on the cross our abandonment by God.

"The Word became flesh": this is the event that God could risk. If we are contented and pleased with our life, happy in our cosy nook, we don't understand these words. But if we think of man's awful desperation and depths as they appear constantly in world-history and of all man's upward striving out of abysses that always become so much greater, then we can understand what is meant by "the Word became flesh". Into this bottomless abyss eternal mind, eternal clarity, eternal understanding – in fact, the divine *Logos* himself – ventured.

In his radical decision, he declares that all this is not to be regarded as the unavoidable margin of the divine, something that unfortunately emerges just at the point where God's splendour begins to shine out, but it is all assumed by God himself, because it can be assumed and redeemed; because in fact life can appear in and at death, riches in poverty, abundance in emptiness, bliss in grief, freedom in servitude. How? This is the miracle of grace and the miracle of faith. When these things take place, faith and grace can perceive it: the fall into the abyss is suddenly filled with grace, becoming a fall into the blessed abyss of God, where death is somehow filled with life. Think of the beatitudes in the sermon on the mount, where Jesus says just the same thing: that those who mourn are blessed, that the poor are rich (Mt 5:3-12).

Let us consider also the fact that a child is born. Jesus, the eternal *Logos*, also took on himself individually a history, with all its surprises, its turns and restrictions. Consider the stable, the angels' song, and consider the words of scripture: "Mary kept all these things, pondering them in her heart" (Lk 2:19).

The incarnation continues. For what was then assumed, what is assumed, is each day freshly assumed. In this assumption of the non-divine into the innermost possessions, into the innermost reality of God himself, we too are assumed, taken up into the life of God. If God himself possesses an earthly reality as his own and if this reality cannot be conceived at all without the world, without its environment, without human surroundings, then already in the *Logos* himself through his incarnation the world and humanity are assumed, we are assumed. We belong to him, in the unity of the hypostatic union we have already been accepted by God; looking to Jesus, we have really only one thing to do: to accept ourselves. Then we shall have assumed what God has assumed, taken up, redeemed, declared definitive. Therein we have found God himself in his blessed incomprehensibility.

8 THE HIDDEN LIFE OF JESUS

As Ignatius suggests (134, 271), it is a good thing to make a meditation on the hidden life of Jesus. The assumption of human life by Jesus, the eternal Word of the Father, necessarily means that whatever belongs otherwise to human existence belongs also to this human life of the eternal Word of God: the ordinary, the normal, the commonplace, the boringly repetitive, what all men have in common, what is insignificant. This is assumed and is therefore confirmed. Hence we see also in the gospels how three phases of Jesus' life are clearly distinguished: the hidden life (as we usually describe it, but it would perhaps be better to say: the normal and average life, the life belonging to and imposed on all men equally); the public life, beginning with his baptism; then, finally and clearly separated (in the gospels also) from the rest, the Lord's passion.

We shall have to admit that the evangelists are only marginally interested in the personal pre-history of the messiah. They have not much to tell of the story of Jesus before his baptism, before his public appearance as teacher in Israel. This again is obvious: there is not much to be said about it. But this very silence, since it is a silence about a period in the life of the Son of God in our flesh, is itself of supreme importance. Silence here becomes audible and striking.

The fact that the canonical gospels – by contrast with the apocryphal – have almost nothing to report on this first period is significant for us. The assumption of the ordinariness of human life, the assumption of "the form of a servant" (Phil 2:7), is decisive; not much can be said about that. If we may say so, this little is our salvation. What Jesus says of himself in his public life is what he was in his normal, hidden life, and this is what has redeemed us, what reached its peak in the cross. For there too death, simply as death, as it comes to everyone, decisively, and not merely as an extraordinary death on the cross, is the event of the redemption.

The hidden and the public life of Jesus reach their consummation in this death, and are combined in it; but this again shows that the hidden life, of which nothing can be said, is of essential importance for salvation. While his preaching is nothing more than the announcement of the fact that the eternal *Logos* assumed human existence under the veil of the commonplace, this also comes silently to the fore in the unobtrusiveness of his hidden life.

1. *Growth*

If we wanted to define the hidden life of Jesus as the form of our life, we might say that there is an explicit statement about its growth in Luke 2:52: "And Jesus increased . . ."

You know of course that the question of Jesus' human consciousness is again regarded today as presenting considerable difficulty to theology and exegesis. We cannot and need not go into it here in a meditation. But while recognising as present in Jesus from the first (as another aspect of the hypostatic union) this basic cognitive relationship to the Father, this knowledge of his union with the eternal Word in the depths of his human nature, we must also recognise that just this ultimate, original, basic condition of his existence is not the same as reflex knowledge of an individual object and that it does not exclude, but positively involves, a real growth, the real acceptance of the phases of human life. Each phase of our life is there sanctified and accepted, its possibilities confirmed, and referred to the later phase. For every phase of human life – as the hidden life of Jesus shows – has its own, unique, irreplaceable importance and cannot be absolutised, but must obediently give way to the later phase.

Our childhood is certainly behind us. But something of this hidden, growing life always remains of supreme importance for us. For every man until he dies is constantly faced by the problem of setting aside an earlier period of life in the right way, without denying it, and willingly and obediently accepting the later phase of life as it comes.

But take a look at the way people live. How many want to remain children and in a sense refuse to grow up; how many want to remain active and refuse to accept old age. The hidden life is expressly a life of growth (Lk 2:40), of change, and thus also a life of surprise, of a life that could not be planned in advance. We can make plans for later periods of our life, we can decide according to our feelings, we can prepare and adapt ourselves, but no one really knows how he will feel later. Such a period always offers surprises; it must be faced in the right way from the start (since each period comes only once). This is the noble art of life, which cannot be taught and therefore has to be sought as a grace from God: an art in which we have to trust in God.

Just think: You took on the priesthood as a final decision for life. You can no longer go back on this decision; you must sustain it through all the periods of life that you do not and cannot yet know. If we wanted to make this ignorance an argument against the finality of a life's decision, indissoluble marriage, perpetual vows, the priesthood, it would mean that we could always undertake a responsibility, a task, simply in the light of the experience of a particular moment.

This inner brittleness, this inner discontinuity, this "I don't know what I shall be doing tomorrow", this unwillingness to accept responsibility for a later stage, is more or less typical of modern times and modern men. Here we should and must have the courage to live another life, the life of inner continuity, of "growth", of the inner relatedness of the different phases and periods of life to one another and also to the unity of life: with its "Yes", with its decision and with what comes later, although we do not yet know it.

Experience of the apostolate at thirty is something quite different from the experience at sixty. The life of prayer is likewise different at different phases. How we experience, suffer and endure celibacy differs with each individual phase. Can we nevertheless say "Yes"? We can. Why? Because God has guaranteed through his Spirit in the church to sustain us with his grace, if only we do our part, if we manage to imitate and to realise afresh the one, continuous growth of Christ simply as man, unfolding it in the unity of one life.

This is really possible. Of course it requires a great confidence in God. We are invited to be so confident, to be confident that we can take on a way of life which stands up to the test of a situation arising later, a situation which could not be anticipated or first tried out; to be confident in the God-given, genuine continuity and homogeneity of our individual life, which of course will have its crises of growth, crises which may involve very harsh new decisions and also up to a point very different ways of life in the particular phases. But through the Spirit of the church, through the truth of the gospel, we have the guarantee that, if we are faithful to God's grace, this transition to what cannot yet be foreseen will lead to a genuine, rich, humanly full life. Obviously it will be in such a way that the death of Christ, sacrifice and self-denial also have their essential place in this life. Without this will to the cross of Christ, this inner continuity of the one life as it is unfolded in different phases could not be maintained.

2. *Able to wait*

Jesus' hidden life tells us something about the growth of human life, tells us likewise something about being able to wait. We might say that for each of us our longest period of waiting is now behind us: it consisted in the years of training for the priesthood. There were some who certainly had to wait long enough for the priesthood. But first of all we might ask ourselves whether we really waited or whether we cut short the period of waiting, not by terminating it too soon, but by introducing diversions and making life more pleasant. Then the question arises whether we might not still have something to make good. But let us assume that we could say before God that we waited patiently, then there is still something to learn from these thirty years of our Lord's long waiting for his real calling:

this remains the foremost example for us and for our life in future.

There is always something still to be achieved in our life; we don't simply dispose of it, but to a large extent we have to go out to accept it. The acceptance of what God plans is our life's work. To that extent we are always waiting throughout our life for what is still to come, what is assigned to us, what we cannot plan. In the last resort we are waiting for the death which God gives us, which we can never anticipate, even if we live to be eighty. Consequently this remaining open, this patient waiting, is part of the basic structure of the christian life: that is why Jesus, who really seemed to enter on the scene quite by chance and at an already advanced age, was able to wait in an almost uncanny fashion.

We know nothing about the exact details of this part of Jesus' life in regard to his vocation, although there too a genuine, human waiting and maturing was possible in spite of his basic knowledge of the Father and the task there opened up of the redemption of the world. The "how" has not been made known to us. The more you think of the fact that Jesus knew and wanted to know in a reflex, objective-propositional way about his future calling, so much the more surprising does it seem that he waited so long; and the more you stress the genuine self-development of the man, the more you see again that he did wait. This of course is very general and abstract; it would have to be concretely applied and in fact in regard to the dual question: when can I not wait, and where do I wait no longer, because I have in a sense already reached the end? It is the same mistake in both cases.

3. Poverty

We are told expressly of the poverty of Christ (2 Cor 8:9). Poverty again not so much as ascetic practice, as a work of supererogation, but poverty as acceptance of the normal, ordinary, average conditions of life, as they were then for a man of that time, in that dimension. The unobtrusive, the normal, the average, even of poverty, is more significant and important for us than a Franciscan passion for an extraordinary poverty which is difficult to carry out at the present time when it is impossible to escape the flood of consumer goods. Nevertheless, the important thing is to understand the spirit of this hidden poverty of Jesus' life and to have the courage to practise it in our life. It is at this point that the very real decision comes for patient and unobvious, unsensational acceptance of a priestly life which can certainly be described as poverty in Jesus' sense.

4. Work

Work plays a large part in the hidden life of Jesus (Mt 13:15; Mk 6:3). He appears as the carpenter's son and as carpenter himself, manual worker, workman, or however you like to translate the word. Jesus was a kind of priest-worker. He worked, he adapted himself quite naturally and unobtrusively to this milieu. To say that he adapted himself however is not strictly true. In spite of his knowledge of his divine sonship, he belongs to the place where his human life began. All that he has in this way, he experiences in the light of this obvious, human, earthly origin; he was probably not at all surprised by this, he did not feel it to be a special condescension.

We must only look back to this spontaneous acceptance of his ordinary, hidden life: it is we who are surprised at our life, who are tempted to protest against it, who don't feel that we can take it for granted. He sustained everything completely naturally and spontaneously precisely in the light of his knowledge of his divine sonship. If you were to use this – so to speak – as a mental lever to decide to what extent Jesus wondered about his situation, you would misunderstand this divine sonship. For you need only ask: What other way of life would have been better suited to the Son of God? If he had been a rich man, a scholar, if he had been a great statesman or one of the world's great artists, these things would still be trivial by comparison with the divine sonship.

If the Son of God coming into the flesh of this world, the most ordinary, the most average, the most normal, the most insignificant thing is what is most bearable, because any sort of documentary proof and documentation of this infinite dignity and reality would have been so inadequate as to be simply absurd. The Son of God in the dimensions of human reality cannot be demonstrated by reference to learning, to scholarship and politics and the like. In a way all that we can do is to be human, an average human being, taking the human condition for granted: what is behind all this we can say quickly, briefly, modestly, and we can die. We can do what Jesus in fact did.

5. *Obedience*

Jesus lived in obedience. You must not rush to find parallels to this in the obedience of a religious order; his obedience was that which obviously belongs to a growing, maturing, human life. It is the obedience which means patient and spontaneous respect for those fixed situations in human life that cannot be altered. It is the kind of obedience given to political authority. Jesus is obedient to his parents, he fits in naturally with the religious setting of his people, of his time, although he can certainly be conscious that he is not tied to it, that he is "lord of the sabbath" (Mt 12:8). But it is almost horrifying to see how these things are taken into this hidden life without any sense of repugnance, as if it were simply not worth while to overthrow them in a violent revolution. In all these things, circumstances, structures of his life, as they are, he is obedient; he is patient and respects them. This is his obedience.

6. *Prayer*

The next thing that we know expressly from scripture about Jesus' hidden life is that he prayed (Mk 1:35; Lk 3:21; 6:12). It should be said that this is obvious, that it is a direct consequence of the hypostatic union. But scripture also shows us that the Son of God was the very person who lived his religious life also within the framework of the religion of his people, within the framework of this very problematic institutional religion (cf, for instance, his going up to Jerusalem mentioned in Lk 2:41f.).

7. *Hidden life – contemplative life*

There is a hiddenness of christian existence which in all the daily routine is the deeper ground of what we may call the hidden life of Jesus or our hidden life. We read that "your life is hid with Christ in God" (Col

3:3); that we are dead to the world through baptism (Rom 6:6); that "our commonwealth is in heaven" (Phil 3:20); that faith is 'the assurance of things hoped for, the conviction of things not seen" (Heb 11:1); that Moses as our example endured both the invisible and the palpable (Heb 11:27). All this relates to a hiddenness of the christian life behind and prior to this hiddenness of a life as we normally understand it.

What is most real in our life can be grasped only by faith. There is certainly something like a genuine experience of faith, but what is really important in the life of the christian and particularly of the priest is hidden and can be possessed and to some extent experienced in faith and only in faith. This is a decisive feature in our situation as christians, as priests. We live – so to speak – into the hidden mystery of God. The centre of our life is something we cannot control, cannot directly experience or enjoy. We have our focal point in something that simply cannot be proved in secular terms. This necessarily belongs to our existence and we are constantly, sometimes harshly and radically questioned in our lives as priests: whether we are really dead to the world; whether we have risen in such a way that we set our minds on things that are above (Col 3:1–4), reflect on them, make them the centre of our existence; whether we really believe that the invisible, the incomprehensible, is the more reliable or whether we are in fact people who prefer the one bird in the hand to two in the bush. The christian and the priest is essentially the person for whom God's still unfulfilled promise is distinctly more real, closer to the source of existence than all the rest that man can grasp, produce, enjoy.

The seclusion of Jesus' life is the expression and the realisation of this hiddenness of what is most real in Jesus and in our life, in the "form of a servant" (Phil 2:7). In other words, what we have hitherto described as the hidden life of Jesus, what we have designated as a structural principle of our life, is merely the application and realisation of a living faith that what is most real in our existence cannot be directly grasped and yet is also what is absolutely essential to us, for our basic attitude, decisions and way of life.

It is from this standpoint that we really begin to see what is happening in our normal, average, regular life. This seclusion – that is, normal, commonplace and often boring life – is the climate in which the hidden supernatural life of the christian is practised; it is the way in which faith in the hidden God as the centre of our life must be realised. From this standpoint too we understand what really matters in our hidden life: unsensational life, the life of obedience, of regularity, of simplicity, of a certain calmness and austerity, a certain continuity and solid planning. All this is a yardstick to test our achievement of a life of faith.

Of course such an average, normal life involves no small degree of danger: the danger of sinking into apathy, of misinterpreting this life as if it were that of the average, faint-hearted, commonplace individual. This is not what is meant by the life of seclusion as the practice of faith in the importance of the absolutely hidden life of grace, but it can be so misunderstood. This is involved in the human condition. A figure which is really the embodiment of a particular mind has its own objectivity, its own stable laws, inseparable from this mind existing in this shape and under these laws, and therefore the figure can be transformed into something quite different. The hard simplicity of a normal life, of someone who can live without sensations, who can deny himself, make sacrifices, be silent, can be turned into the cheap mediocrity of someone who does not undertake any great venture, who is timid and avoids all that has to do with greatness. Such a life can be changed into a life that seeks a substitute for austerity in meaner things, to compensate in fact for the greater goods which we have renounced.

Alongside this life of seclusion, then, what we call the contemplative life would have to be considered as the content of the hidden life with Christ in God. We shall have to return to this topic in connection with the question of the priesthood. But the theme also comes within the scope of the present meditation. The content of our inner life is precisely life with Christ in God: the life of the Spirit of God in us, the life of patience, fidelity, love, prayer, of looking for and expectation of eternal life.

You may ask yourselves whether and how with you this common life in the sense of ordinary life has remained a hidden life with Christ in God: how far we are involved in the present-day loss of the spirit of prayer, how far we suffer from the reduction of humanity today to a mass of individuals, from the craving for external excitement. All these things are possible today to a greater extent than they were formerly and therefore present a greater danger. This does not mean that we have to condemn the present time and its mode of life, but we must see soberly and clearly what are the dangers we have to face today and how we feel in regard to the contemplative life as hidden life with Christ in God: then we must adapt ourselves accordingly, in conformity with the present time, but also in a christian, supernatural, priestly way, in order so to come to terms with the present time as to be demonstrating through our life that it is possible to be a christian and a priest today without trying to escape from our age.

Let us ask God to enable us to understand and imitate the hidden life of Jesus, to see our life as such an imitation of the hidden life of Christ and therefore not merely to live outwardly in a regular, normal and relevant way, but also to discover in it the Spirit of Christ, who is the very meaning of this life and without whom this life would be nothing but regulated, institutionalised boredom. This is not what our life should be, nor does it need to be so. Why? Because the Spirit of Christ, poured out in our hearts (Rom 5:5), can grant us a life in this outward form which already anticipates eternal life so far as it is now possible.

9 THE CATHOLIC PRIESTHOOD

In this meditation we shall try to develop – not perhaps very systematically – some ideas on the nature of the priesthood.

1. *Mediating functionary of a total religious system*

First of all a very secular and realistic reflection on the priest, seen from an empirical-sociological viewpoint. If the church is a visible society – and this is what the catholic church asserts, against all protestant heresies – then she has a social embodiment, and this can certainly – even though only analogically – be described in general sociological categories and terms. The same holds in a true, though provisional, sense for the priesthood. If we were to be carried away by any kind of idealism and did not see this aspect, it could lead only to disillusionment and to dangers for our priesthood.

If we consider the priest from a sociological-empirical standpoint, we might describe him as a mediating functionary of a total – but not totalitarian – religious system. The church understands herself undoubtedly as a total system, integrating and seeking to integrate (in spite of all distinctions between the natural and supernatural orders) more or less all spheres of life into itself, which exercises authority over all these spheres, at least *ratione peccati*. Hence we can certainly consider the church (particularly the catholic church with her absolute claims, which she has and must have) sociologically and phenomenonologically as a religious system and define her as a total system. Then the priest is an office-holder, a functionary, within this total religious system: as ordinary priest, as priest of the second order, a mediating functionary who in any case has superiors above him.

In the first place then, regarded from the standpoint of this world, the priest is a kind of dependent official by contrast to someone who practises a profession. Through the priesthood we enter into an hierarchical body with clearly defined ranks and a definite structure of its own. This structure is given us in advance. We have to adapt ourselves to it. In this sense therefore we are officials of a *societas perfecta*. This is an absolutely correct definition of our priestly life and existence and, even though merely external and provisional, it must not be overlooked. We belong to a larger system: while being dependent on those above us and those below, we have a particular way of life, which exists before we make our own decision; we are in this sense therefore dependent officials.

All the peculiarities, all the mental-sociological necessities and dangers of such a state of life, with which we have to come to terms, arise out of these facts. Because we are officials of such a social-religious system, we have a way of life given us in advance.

This is not self-evident: for the priest is nevertheless plainly and simply the religious man. He is and must be the one who is driven by the Spirit. He must shape and plan his life from an innermost personal centre. But – unlike a hermit or a free charismatic – he can do so only by incorporating this innermost spiritual vocation of his into this officially pre-organised system. It is obvious that this will involve tensions, problems, pain and sacrifice. In this life of a dependent official within the church as a total religious system, as distinct from that of another official belonging to a different social structure, the priest necessarily no longer has any private life. The official of a structure that is not so totally religious can put part of his time, his strength, his interest, at the disposal of this social structure and reserve the rest to himself. There is a prior agreement between the social structure and the functionary about how much of his life the latter will place at the disposal of the former.

From the very nature of the situation this cannot be the case with the functionary of a total religious system. In a sense, he is always on duty. Of course he has a private life: he sleeps, eats, has certain hobbies which offend nobody, and so on. But this is not a reserved sphere of life: it has to be justified once again by this mission, in which he devotes himself wholly and entirely to this religious structure with its absolute claims. We cannot say from the first that we would like this period for our free time, that we will not give up this hobby, that this pleasure or this comfort is un-doubtedly ours, and that we shall put at the disposal of the church and our priesthood only what is then left over (even though this may be a great deal). This won't work. In the light of this sociological aspect of his life, the priest must clearly understand that he belongs body and soul, with all that he is, to this church, to her task, to her mission, her work, her destiny, and can never dissociate himself from these things. A statesman can never say that his working day is finished, that all his tasks can be left aside after office hours. He must perhaps have some recreation, perhaps do something else, but he does all this only in the light of his mission as a great statesman. The same applies *mutatis mutandis* to our priestly life.

2. *The risk of institutionalising religions*

If the priest, seen from the outside and sociologically, is the mediating functionary in such a total religious structure, then – since as a man of religion, as a priest, he lives in a *societas perfecta* at the service of the divine – the risk of institutionalising religion exists. The priesthood is religion given an institutional form, with definite tasks and goals. The priest does not pray simply in an outburst of enthusiasm or idealism, he has to "complete" a part of the breviary each day; it is not only when he is seized by the Spirit of God that he celebrates the eucharist, he says mass every day; he does not speak merely out of the warmth of his heart, he has to take classes, he has to talk about God even when he finds this boring.

All this belongs to the priestly life: as the life of a functionary of a *societas perfecta religiosa*, it is necessarily institutionalised religion. Anyone who felt that he could have nothing to do with this religious institutionalising could no longer be a christian. As priests we must accept the fact that we have to allow for and cope with considerably more of such institutionalising than is expected of the laity. This must not be allowed to kill the inner vitality of our religious life. We must accept the risk of such an institutionalising with trust in God and in the power of his Spirit. This Spirit has shaped his institutional, legal embodiment and guarantees constantly to cope with its limitations and rigidity. What we accept of priestly, established institutionalism in our religious and priestly life is bearable and, if it is achieved in the right way, can even be and remain a very substantial fostering, preservation, realisation and objectification of the inner spirit of the priesthood. Of course we must see the dangers of such an institutionalising of religion, in which our priesthood is involved: the danger of over-exertion, of the unauthentic, of routine, of feeble compromise, of perversion of values, with the result that religious life then becomes a means to private life, becomes stereotyped, outwardly clericalised, the practice of a priestly life no longer in accordance with its spirit, since it is presumably deliberately over-taxed through this institutional element.

Of course it is difficult to say office every day at all meaningfully, to celebrate mass daily as participation in the last supper of Jesus Christ, as the proclamation of his death, the taking up of his cross, as the anticipated celebration of eternal life. The danger exists of exercising this ministry in a routine way, unauthentically, merely bureaucratically, in a purely external institutional fashion. We must constantly protect ourselves against this correctly and skilfully, with an intelligent psychology and by avoiding unreasonable over-exertion. God will certainly give us his grace.

3. *Continuation of Christ's priesthood*
We are asking what is the inner reality, what is the real meaning of such a sociological phenomenon which we must face soberly and clearly if we want to become and to be priests. It is – briefly – the continuation of the priesthood of Christ. Christ in his unity of God and man, as the grace of humanity in self-achievement and

self-utterance, is plainly and simply priest; as personal agent, he is the primal sacrament fulfilled, inseparably united with the reality signified, primal sign that the infinite grace of God, which is God himself, has been bestowed on mankind eschatologically, victoriously, effectively; that is to say that Christ imparts himself through his being, through the self-achievement of his divine-human reality and through the self-utterance in which he proclaims what he is. The church and the priest must be seen from this standpoint, the priest however in the unity of the cultic and prophetic elements.

In the light of the old testament the catholic priest is a unity of cultic-levitical priesthood and the non-institutional prophetic calling. These two functions, separated in the old testament for very profound but provisional reasons, were united in Jesus Christ. The catholic priest achieves this unity of prophetical, ever-new, incalculable priesthood, called to topical proclamation of the word, and the permanent, enduring cultic priesthood. At the same time, it must also be seen that the catholic priest does not continue these two functions of the eternal high priest, united in Jesus Christ, in such a way that this high priest Jesus Christ abandons his functions and disappears into the silent eternity of God, but in such a way that he is in a true sense merely the instrument of this one permanent high priest Jesus Christ. Consequently, he is only the one who can offer the sacrifice of Christ in time and space, here and now, but without multiplying it, even though the cultic celebration is multiplied; and he can speak and accomplish in his prophetic ministry only the word of Jesus Christ and no other, new word surpassing this, but can only be the ministerial actuality of this final word of Jesus Christ – which in the last resort is Christ himself.

From this standpoint we must also observe how this personally recruited prophetic priesthood of the new covenant establishes a way of life. There is a new, special mode of existence in relation to other christians and distinct from theirs, which directly sets up a state of life for the priest as prophet. By expounding his word, implementing his cultic mandate, he links this prophetic element of course with the cultic priesthood: this the catholic priest possesses in so far as he performs this expounding, proclaiming, defending, preaching, persuading function of interpreting this efficacious sacramental word in his mission, the mission which drives him out of his native, secular situation. Because he must proclaim – *opportune, importune* – the word of Christ at a point where he does not belong in virtue of his natural, secular condition, the ordained priesthood in the catholic church acquires a very special character, distinguishing it from the life of the normal christian.

Consider all these things in connection with other words of scripture which describe this essence of the christian priesthood. He is the envoy, the representative of Christ and the Father, steward of the mysteries of God (1 Cor 4:1); he is the fellow-worker of God (1 Cor 3:9). It is said of the apostles, the first priests, that they are Christ's friends (Jn 15:15), that they bear witness to Christ (Ac 1:8), that in a particularly impressive way they are the heralds, the preachers of the word of God (Rom 15:16). Always and everywhere among all nations and at all times, they preach *metanoia*, the advent of the kingdom of God. They preach the good news, by Christ's mandate, as his envoys (Eph 3:8). Their task is described as the ministry of the word. They are the dispensers of the sacraments (2 Cor 5:18); they are called teachers of the nations, fishers of men (Mt 4:19). They are described as fathers of souls, whom they beget in their supernatural life in Christ Jesus through the gospel.

4. *Servants of the community*

Here is something to which I would like to draw your attention. Priests – as the name suggests – are the elders, *presbyteroi*, in the community, for the community and from the community (Ac 11:30; Rom 12:8; Phil 1:1; 2 Tim 1:6). By and large, however, priests today are not of the older generation in the sense of biological age; but this relationship of service to the community is of the essence of the catholic priesthood. Although the priest's mandatory powers are given him by Christ and not given to the laity, these powers are given in a ministerial sense, since Christ loves and wills the community of the redeemed, of the justified, of those united in love. The church has an existence and structure prior to her official hierarchical constitution; and, however much the hierarchical structure belongs to her necessary being, founded by Christ, it exists in fact because this church is and must be and because Christ has redeemed and called together mankind into the community of believers, of the justified and redeemed.

We do not obtain our official powers democratically from the multitude: we have them because there is and must be the holy community of God in Jesus Christ.

All these functions therefore are ministerial functions. In the last resort those in the highest place are not pope and bishops, not priests, but those who believe most radically and love God most radically in Jesus Christ. First and last is and remains this inner hierarchy of holiness. All juridical, hierarchical structure has merely a ministerial and sacramental function in regard to this church of the Spirit, as Augustine in his day explained at length. We must always be aware of this in our calling. Even today we constantly hear from the faithful the reproach of clerical exclusiveness, of clerical arrogance, of clerics claiming always to know better. These attitudes are contrary to our nature as priests. We are merely ministers of reconciliation (2 Cor 5:18), "ministers of their joy" (2 Cor 1:24), those who deliver another's message and can do nothing else but – to quote Ignatius – "to unite the creature directly with its creator".

In the *Acts of the Martyrs* there is an account of the martyrdom of Bishop Felix of Thibiuca. There we read, at the end: "Bishop Felix, raising his eyes to heaven, said in a clear voice: 'God, I thank you. I have lived 56 years in this world. I have kept my virginity, I have upheld the gospels, I have preached the faith and the truth. Lord God of heaven and earth, Jesus Christ, I bend my neck as victim to you who remain for ever.' "[1] At the close of our priestly life, by whatever kind of death it comes, we should be able to pray in these brave words.

[1] R. Knopf–G. Krüger, *Ausgewählte Märtyrerakten*, Tübingen, 1929³, p 91.

10 PRIESTLY OFFICE AND PERSONAL HOLINESS

One point of the last meditation is of great importance for the correct understanding of the priesthood: it is the problem of office and person, of official mandate and personal holiness. Of course we know from what we were taught about asceticism that the priest ought to be holy and virtuous, that he ought to be a shining example to the faithful entrusted to his guidance. Nevertheless, it is a good and useful thing to consider more closely this relationship between official mandate and personal holiness: for – in spite of all exhortation to asceticism – under the influence of the idea of the *opus operatum* and official, mandatory powers, of an anti-Donatist defensive reaction, we are always tempted to see office, priesthood and its powers independently of our personal life.

At least from Augustine's time or from the time of the reformation, the catholic church has been apparently the church of objective powers, the church of the *opus operatum*, which is independent of the holiness of the ministers. We stress the fact that a person does not lose his membership of the church as a result of his own personal sinfulness, that the "objective powers" continue to be active even in the sinful priest. We train the faithful to appreciate the mass and the sacraments, even the sacramentals, without regard to the person who undertakes these sacred actions, without regard to the degree of the priest's holiness. Behind this is the objectivist, anti-Donatist feeling, which is right up to a point, but can mislead us into over-looking the firm, intrinsic unity of person and office. We need only look more closely at our moral theology in its lesser and finer ramifications to see that there are a number of problems here which have not been properly considered and that there certainly remain objectively false deviations from the right conception which combines subjective, existential religious activity on the one hand and objective accomplishment of the institutional requirements of the church on the other.

1. *Love decides*

Ultimately, what counts for God is simply and solely the personal, freely given love of the individual. The love which he brings about through his Holy Spirit and which cannot be brought about through anyone except the Holy Spirit of God's grace and the wholly personal unique freedom of the individual. All the rest – church, institution, sacraments, *opus operatum*, all that is regulated and institutionalised – is nothing but a means to this personal commitment, willed by God, objectively necessary and completely justified. Objective holiness of the church too in the truth of her proclamation, in the *opus operatum* of her sacraments, in the divine law which she makes her own, in her persistence to the end, is nothing but the means to this one end: that there should be believing, loving, hoping, loyal human beings, united to God.

This holds obviously for us too in so far as we are not only christians, but also priests. This does not mean at all that these two aspects are in the last resort fundamentally opposed, that we can have the one only by sacrificing the other, just as – if you like – the Donatists or Wyclif, or Hus and the protestants, thought. It remains true that there is subordination, a hierarchy of values which is important for practical questions; and in this genuine catholic hierarchy of values, love, grace, inner justification, inward commitment in freedom to God are superordinated to office, sacraments, institution, to any objective sum-total of obligations. This is seen still more clearly, if we reflect on the holiness of the church rightly understood.

2. *Holy church*

When we say that the church is the permanently holy church, we do not mean merely – as in the old covenant – that the objective institution of the church and her truth, her proclamation, is true, her sacraments are valid, her institution is permanent; but we mean also that God himself, through his predestining, efficacious grace sees to it that the church, in her members as a whole, is also always the subjectively holy church: for this is just what God wants in regard to this eschatological community of believers.

A church which was only objectively, in its institutions and its proclamation, in accordance with God's will, and in this sense holy, would not be the church of Jesus Christ, the church as eschatological reality. For it is simply and solely through Jesus Christ, because of the last days, because of the absolute, victorious power of his definitive redemption, that a church is founded which, in the power of the Holy Spirit and his grace, overtaking, not destroying, but sustaining freedom, permanently provides for the church in her members to be the subjectively holy church. But this means that the danger which both Donatists and anti-Donatists seem to fear will not arise: namely, that one day the subjectively holy church and the objectively holy church – regarded in their whole reality – might fall apart.

There cannot really be a discrepancy so great as to involve the co-existence of objectively valid sacrament, objectively valid authority, truth rightly proclaimed on the one hand, and unholy, unbelieving holder of these mandates on the other. This danger exists only for the individual as individual in the church, but not for the church as a whole. This is why, particularly after Vatican I, the church is necessarily bound to appear as the subjectively holy and – in the inexhaustible abundance of her holiness so understood – as the sign raised up to the nations, and the permanent place for the practical experience of her divine foundation.

3. *Unity of existential and institutional holiness*

From all this we clearly perceive that there is and must be a unity of existential and institutional holiness, necessary first of all for the church as a whole, a unity indispensable to the church, produced by God through the power of his grace. This unity of existential and institutional elements, necessary for the church, is therefore obviously required of the individual priest. Only when he realises this unity to a significant degree is the priest the person he must be. The priesthood of · the church is completely the priesthood of holy men and not of holders of office for whose meaning and importance this personal holiness is a matter of indifference. If the latter were the case it would lead to an absurd situation in which we could say that the sacraments only have to be valid in themselves, although of course they are fortunately also often fruitful.

The sacrament as such is defined in the light of its significance and of the grace it really imparts to the individual human being. It is of course easy to see the reasons why, as *opus operatum*, it can also at times be valid and yet not fruitful; but this is a sacramental situation which, from the very nature of the sacrament, ought not to exist and ought not to be allowed to exist. To this extent, the merely institutional priest of the *opus operatum*, who does not fill this with the whole force of his personality, thus sustaining what he does, preaches, ministers and so on, is not the person he ought to be.

It is not as if God in a moral ruling, for reasons more or less of edification, also requires holiness on the part of the bearer of his official, mandatory powers, because this looks better, because it is anyway more fitting; this existential holiness of the bearer of objective powers is something required by his very nature in the holy church of the eschatological situation, and absolutely required in the indestructible and also subjectively holy church. This does not mean that the office would cease to exist if this requirement were not satisfied, but it does mean that this requirement really corresponds also to the innermost nature of office in the church and is not here an additional moral requirement on Christ's part.

Some conclusions emerge now which we can think out for ourselves. I have already pointed out that Paul does not think at all simply and primarily in terms of the objective administration of the sacraments: properly speaking, his thought is dominated by the proof of the dynamism of the Spirit, by his preaching, in which his whole person is existentially involved (2 Cor 4:2, Eph 3:7) and only because of this is not indeed authorised, but becomes credible for the person who is to hear it. Here you see already how in fact it lies in the essence of priesthood to give expression in the priestly calling to this requirement of personal holiness; how understandable it is therefore when the Western priest wants and is also urged by the church to be more than a mere "massing priest", only taking care of the continuation of objective cult and objective administration of the sacraments in the church.

11 PRIESTHOOD AND RELIGIOUS LIFE

If we consider our priesthood in a religious order, a relationship between these two basic factors must undoubtedly exist in our life; at the same time, this relationship is a problem, at least in the first place.

The problem consists in the fact that it is neither simple nor obvious for us to see these two factors in a unity. For one thing, the orders today are being largely levelled out in regard to each other. By comparison with former times, their ascetic, their intellectual and personal level has not declined; but in their style of life and form of life – although differently in different countries – they have come much closer to one another.

The universal canon law, which holds for all the orders, imposes a degree of equality which did not exist in former times. The teaching of the particular orders is no longer, as formerly, a matter that concerns each order in itself. Theological doctrines associated with particular orders are certainly relaxed, if they still exist at all. Today the intellectual, theoretical, scientific and even pastoral fronts, up to a point, run right across the orders. Many a Jesuit will find himself more in agreement over a large area of pastoral ministry with many a Dominican than with some of his Jesuit colleagues. These are simply facts, which cannot be disputed. In this sense the orders have lost something of their special character and come closer to one another in a general levelling out.

Thus in spite of all the remaining differences, in spite of the justified, necessary individuality of the particular orders, which is salutary for the church, these things are no longer so strikingly obvious, so that from this standpoint it is not so easy for a person to decide to which order he has a vocation. Even if each one has chosen this community more or less naturally and spontaneously, this blurring of the distinction between the mental physiognomies of the particular orders still raises a problem. In this way what is common – the priesthood as the real and central factor – necessarily comes much more strongly to the fore. The important thing is to see this fact without prejudice and see clearly that it would be foolish, perverse, stupid, unjust and disloyal, to want to draw the conclusion that we must be cool and reserved in regard to the order which we happen to have entered. Nevertheless, in this way the priesthood in our life necessarily and automatically acquires a greater, more distinct, centrality than the religious life. This however must not be taken to mean that we are casting envious glances at the secular priesthood, as if we had to regard this as the real thing and the religious life as offering us at best common catering arrangements.

There are in addition problems of adapting the old orders to the new age. Our times are different from those of a hundred years ago. This change is being brought about at an enormously accelerated rate; it is therefore obvious that it will be hard to come to terms with these changes of a social and intellectual character. It would be both stupid and naive to think that this problem could be made easier by founding new orders. In a modest way we might wonder if the newer forms of the religious life or the secular institutes which have arisen up to now have such a fundamentally new and convincing character that the older orders might have to admit that their banners have now been passed to new standard-bearers who carry them more proudly at the head of the regiment, marching into the new age. To this extent the old orders can adapt themselves to the new age, although this adaptation will create problems for the individual: the speed with which they are solved may be too slow for him; he may have to suffer and face harsh sacrifices in his own personal, ascetic and apostolic life.

From this standpoint too the problem of the relationship between the religious life and the priesthood is again raised. Since the priesthood, with its apostolic tasks, its mission in the church, for the church, for the present time, for unbelievers in heathen countries and unbelievers at home, has become an urgent problem, we cannot but ask ourselves whether the mission of the priesthood would not be easier to realise if it were independent of the difficulties of the religious life, of its traditions and somewhat rigid rules.

1. *The unity of the two forms of life*

Having looked at the problem, we must now consider the kind of unity of the two ways of life which would follow appropriately from their nature.

First of all, let us consider this unity as it follows – not necessarily, but appropriately – from the nature of the two factors from the standpoint of the religious life. It would be an absolute misunderstanding of the religious state to regard the religious life in itself as merely a means of striving after personal holiness. In the light of the evangelical counsels, the religious life has an essentially ecclesiological function. It is an essentially apostolic state. There must be the religious life in the church, perhaps in the most diverse forms. That is to say: the state of the realisation of the evangelical counsels, as lived in the social visibility of the church, must necessarily exist in the church.

This state has always existed, since the church must be able to point to those who live the evangelical counsels and thus prove before the world that she is really awaiting the coming of the Lord, that it is she who has shifted the focal point of human existence from intra-mundane experience into grace, into the coming of the Lord. "Come grace, let the world pass away," says the *Didache*: this is something that not only must be lived in the church, but must also belong to what is perceptibly and visibly lived in the church.

The religious state has a witnessing function of living out what is radically christian for man at all times as well as for men of today. Even the most contemplative order in the church has an absolutely apostolic function of witnessing, of confessing the faith, of protesting against a submergence in earthly things, not only by praying, but through its existence and through its way of life. From this standpoint, it is easy to understand that the religious life can at least seek expression in the apostolic element of the priesthood.

On the other hand, we have already said that existential holiness, at least as a requirement, belongs to the nature of priesthood. The priest must bear witness and make his mission credible by his life, not merely by exercising his powers. He is not only the liturgical functionary, but the prophet. He is the real *apostolos*, who is sent and must give testimony. And however much it refers to the testimony of Christ, this testimony is always that of one's own life. In the catholic priest – who is not merely liturgical functionary, but apostle, prophet, envoy, recruiter, missionary – there lies necessarily a tendency towards what is institutionally established and – in the religious life – concretely organised.

There is another thing. When we look to the early church or the new testament, we don't find the priest as individual at all, but the presbyterium. In the primitive constitution of the church, there clearly exists a collegial constitution of the body of leadership in the church, together with, alongside and under the monarchical bishop. We see this already in the relationship of pope to episcopate; we see it likewise in the early church in a relationship then existing between the bishop and his presbyterium. The idea of a collegially constituted group of priests is something that completely corresponds to the nature of the church and the original conception of priesthood in the light of the new testament. It does not follow however that someone who wants to be a priest has to join a group in a college of priests around the bishop.

Seen in the light of a more profound ecclesiology, the orders present structures analogous to that of a diocese. The fact that the highest superiors of an order may be *ordinarii majores*, but not bishops, does not alter this in any way. An order or even – from the standpoint of canon law – a province of an order can be regarded as a kind of personal diocese. It can certainly exercise those functions in the church, for a part of the church and for the totality of the church, which belong to the diocese as such: it is a member competent to act for the church, a member even capable at some point of taking on – not of course quantitatively, but certainly qualitatively – all the tasks to be accomplished in the church.

In other words: the religious life in a community of priests corresponds closely to the presbyteral character with which the priesthood is basically endowed. The fact that this idea found expression at a comparatively late stage in the history of the religious orders does not affect its soundness. These essential features of a living reality come to the fore in accordance with the history of this living institution, visible and juridically constituted; in spite of this delay in time, they are essential features, just as a man must have eyes even though the two-days old embryo still has none.

Hence we can say confidently and with theological accuracy that there is a proper unity of the priesthood and the religious life, not forced or absolutely required, but very obvious from their nature. The existential and collegial aspect of the priesthood seeks expression in the religious life, and on the other hand the ecclesiological function, which belongs to the religious life as such, seeks expression in the priesthood.

2. *Practical conclusions*

First of all, there can be no static relationship between these two factors. The synthesis of the two elements in our life in general and in the life of the individual must constantly be freshly sought and found. Under the circumstances, it is normal and natural that differences should arise, changes come, diverse tendencies appear in this respect in an order. Each of us must feel that he is responsible for the synthesis of the two elements.

There is undoubtedly the danger of becoming a kind of spiritual domestic animal in the community: one who sees the justification of his existence as solely consisting in getting up promptly, taking part in community prayers, and being an exemplary religious, never obtrusive, carefully observing all the rules that are clearly laid down. On the other hand, there are certainly people who feel themselves to be priests, apostles, who develop a keen sense of apostolic mission, but take little or no trouble to see how all this fits in with the unity of the order and with personal life in the order.

Each one of us must ask himself whether we are an order of priests devoted to the apostolate, with courage for fresh adaptation, courage to tackle new problems, to attempt new methods, as befits an order of priests. And each of us must ask himself, even if he were the greatest apostle, how he is to make his naturally small and modest contribution, seriously however and positively, to maintaining the order, the community, in existence.

Furthermore, in spite of the responsibility of the individual for both elements in the synthesis of our religious life as priests, a plurality of types is certainly justified. It is clear of course that this always comes to prevail in practice. One is spiritual director, another preaches; one works as scholar, another writes pious books, and so on. We always have a plurality of working tasks and therefore also of human types in the order. We ought occasionally to reflect on these things.

There is no such thing as a single-stereotype religious. There is a justified plurality of diverse types, since the range of what has been brought into a synthesis here, of religious life and priesthood, simply cannot be lived adequately in one person, but must assume a variety of expressions in the totality of an order. We must not only simply endure these diverse expressions, without envy, humbly, with a critical eye on our own individuality, because we can't get rid of them, but we must recognise them as justified. This antagonistic plurality in the orders – which up to a point is willed by God – in regard to the constitutive factors of the priesthood and the religious life, the apostolate and the world-denying elements, the diversities of nationality, the differences in the generations, which live and have to live together in an order: all this is unavoidable. No one except God and Jesus Christ is Lord over this plurality. In a way, there is no human authority which could adequately survey and direct it.

When history is being made, when within this history there are superiors and subjects, when orders are given and obeyed, the total result of what comes about historically can never be adequately surveyed from any aspect at all. Even the pope, while he is ruling, does not know what point the church will reach after fifty years; to the best of his knowledge and in all conscience he adopts the measures that seem to be required. What the results are, God alone really knows.

This means that we can never expect a time to come when superiors and subjects, when the rule of the order and life as it is lived in practice, will exist together in a heavenly concord and harmony. This cannot and, by God's will, is not meant to exist in this world. We must allow for the fact that there are different tendencies at work which are maintained only with difficulty in the unity of an order, that there are diverse spirits, diverse charisms, in the one order. These things must be tolerated. The individual religious at this point must have the necessary confidence in the unity of the whole, in the guidance of the order's history, which is ultimately under God's control and beyond our vision. He must know that this incalculable, confident self-surrender to the unforeseeable historical significance of an order is also an element of our faith and of the realisation of our hope: faith and hope that we must have in the church and thus too in such essential institutions as religious orders.

12 THE PRIEST AND HIS SUPERIORS

The relationship of the priest to his superiors in church and order is undoubtedly a theme of great importance for the practice of the priestly life, especially for the life of a regular. We can consider the priest's relationship to ecclesiastical and to religious superiors at the same time, not only because these relationships are very similar, but because the order is itself part of the church with its constitutions and its structures approved ecclesiastically and canonically, and because religious obedience is also a part of our ecclesial-priestly obedience, particularly since his higher superiors are ordinaries for the regular as the bishop is for the secular priest.

1. *Obedience as realisation of faith*

First of all, we must consider obedience as an ascetic factor in the religious life as such, as a part of our spiritual life, and – within the order – as a way of achieving that inner assimilation to Christ which we want to realise as an evangelical counsel. This consideration and appreciation of obedience as an ascetic factor – independently of any practical application within the order, which has a common external aim – is undoubtedly the primary aspect under which obedience has been seen historically in the church.

Obedience in the religious life is first of all an evangelical counsel; it has been seen and lived as a way of religious renunciation. What does this mean? Every christian, as a person who is called to a supernatural end, is called to go beyond the human moral virtues of which we have direct experience in this world, in order to grasp in faith as the supreme and central value of his life a virtue which is not accessible to normal experience, but is and can be seen and grasped only in that quite unique act that we call faith: faith – that is – in the invisible, in that which has a supernatural quality. Such a faith cannot be conceived merely as a theoretical assent to a truth revealed by God which of ourselves we could not otherwise reach.

This faith must be existentially realised: the higher value and the absolute centrality of this supernatural end must be given concrete expression. This holds essentially for every christian: for every christian must be a believer, and all salutary faith is more than merely having no objections in theory to the truth of certain propositions. It is the voluntary realisation of these revealed goods of eternal life as central to us, made known and given to us only through revelation. Such an act of faith is by its nature already a kind of renunciation. The personal realisation of the higher values of the supernatural by comparison with merely human good, even moral good, can ultimately be brought about only by the voluntary sacrifice of intramundane good. This renunciation, this sacrifice, then appears as the expression of real faith in the central importance of the supernatural world, of man's destiny, transcending the present world and entering into the life of the triune God in himself.

This is an attitude that belongs to every christian life and need not consist in actively and spontaneously anticipating this renunciation. Through the darkness, the death-trend, the gloom, the pain, the finiteness and the vanity of this life, the christian is faced with the alternative either of despairing or of laying himself open, in an act of trust, faith and love, to God and his incomprehensible decrees. But the christian can deliberately approach this act of his renunciation – which belongs to the essence of christianity – by sacrificing certain positive human goods which it would be completely absurd and even unnatural to sacrifice if this world of God's supernatural self-communication did not exist.

There are circumstances in which a person might be deprived of such goods, even against his will, as a result of the situation in which life had placed him: he might be forced into poverty, he might – as Jesus said – have been born a "eunuch" (Mt 9:12). But quite freely and spontaneously to sacrifice such positive human goods, which essentially represent supreme human values, would be completely absurd, because such a sacrifice would not be at all justified, authorised or outweighed by the anticipation of a still higher value outside the natural order. That is why, incidentally, it is completely superfluous and fundamentally wrong to try to prove in terms of natural ethics – as the traditional moral philosophy did – that virginity, for instance, has a positive significance and value. This does not exclude the possibility that a particular individual in certain conditions might rightly renounce marriage, even within the natural order; but this would be justified only in a situation demanding this renunciation properly speaking against his will, not as something freely undertaken when another choice was open to him.

This is the correct theological interpretation and justification of the evangelical counsels. They are essentially acts of faith, hope and love in regard to those goods which are available only in a supernatural order, in faith, and accessible only in the grace of God. These evangelical counsels as acts of renunciation are author-ised and justified only in regard to these goods, since it would be essentially absurd to sacrifice genuine human values merely for the sake of sacrifice. Renunciation of positive values never has any meaning or justification except for the sake of a higher value.

In this form, the renunciation required by the evan-gelical counsels does not belong simply to any christian life, but what is so realised – as renunciation, as act of faith in regard to the higher goods – is necessarily achieved once also in every other christian life, at least in death. For in death man must allow God to take all those goods which he might have offered more or less spontaneously in an act of faith inspired by the evan-gelical counsels: at death these goods are lost to man and, with the decline of the whole world (as man's world), the world of grace, God's life, emerges and can be grasped only in this way. Faith as total self-surrender, as loving submission of the whole person to God, is always an act of renunciation, because what is at man's disposal – whether in the field of truth or in the field of love – no longer holds that central position or provides that security which it does for someone who does not have to and does not want to believe.

The christian who undertakes obedience in a reli-gious order of course sacrifices only up to a point posi-tive, genuine human values. He renounces and can renounce them only in an act of faith which is a pre-paratory exercise for that act of faith which really involves the whole of human life and is ultimately required of every christian. We need not consider in detail the different dimensions of such (at least relatively) supreme human values as are yielded to God in the renunciation required by the three evangelical counsels. We know that obedience involves the voluntary surrender of some part of man's personal power to dispose of himself, which represents an absolutely positive value. This sort of thing has meaning for mature persons only as part of faith in God, in his love, in his supernatural grace.

Of course, independently of all this, people are always linked together in super- and subordination. But such an obedience is proved to be meaningful by the positive values which are realised through it. When we drive on the correct side of the road and thus avoid collisions, we are in fact obeying the secular authorities, but we also see the reason for it, and this voluntary limitation of our power to dispose of ourselves is rewarded, justified and shown to be good even in this world. It is therefore quite a different kind of obedience from that which is realised in the religious life, where the voluntary limitation of our power of self-disposal is not rewarded in this life. Or, if it is rewarded, it is so only up to a point. It is obvious that when men want to co-operate with each other in an order, rationally and humanly, as comrades – this too is a value that can be proved in human terms – there must be some sort of obedience. There is nothing special about this and therefore obedience of this kind ought not to be glorified by intelligent people, but should be regarded as a simple and obvious everyday fact.

This utilitarian meaning is not central to religious obedience and in the long run cannot justify and sustain obedience either in theory or in the practice of the religious life. It might well be reasonable if we were obedient only in this practical sense, if we were to acknowledge the necessity of co-operation for the sake of the kingdom of God and therefore the necessity of order, of leadership, of adaptation to greater team-work. We would nevertheless at least be in danger of breaking down in our religious obedience. For there can be times when something is required of us, sacrifices are demanded, which cannot be justified in this merely rational and correct way, and then we would no longer see the point of such obedience.

No. There is an evangelical counsel, which is folly to the world, which would be meaningless apart from a radically realised faith. There is a religious obedience which requires us to sacrifice and renounce very positive values. The recompense of this renunciation is one that cannot be known or enjoyed in this world. Humanly speaking at least, it is possible from time to time to find obedience working out in the religious life as something like stupidity, when someone has slipped into it and cannot prove the appropriateness of such obedience in this world. We must appreciate and stick to this sense of obedience as the christian's renunciation and as practice for a radical renunciation which is always imposed in the long run and which the christian will never be spared.

Even if it seems externally that the obedience involving a commitment of faith is not being asked of us, the fact remains that religious life as a whole, in its diffuse, general routine, without the will to this evangelical renunciation, would scarcely present a summons to a life's dedication. The whole of our life stands or falls only by the rules, by the constitutions, by the stereotyping of our life under a common denominator of renunciation, which at most overlooks the boredom, the lack of human feeling, the parsimony. But this is not an advantage and does not indicate any religious achievement: it is merely symptomatic of a deficiency in authentic, human vitality.

If however this vitality is present, then the religious life, particularly in its prosaic routine and normality, provides a challenge to obedience for someone who can bear this – especially if he is alive, humanly authentic and rich – only in a spirit of faith. If, instead of undertaking this task, he were to sink into mediocrity, to cut himself off from real life, to capitulate and compromise, and in this humanly defective state to take on the religious life, he would be like a person who had only managed a lesser calling although he had been meant for a greater; if we endure the religious life only in this way, reducing our claims and sinking into mediocrity, then we have misunderstood the meaning and purpose of obedience.

The fact that obedience is hard for us makes no difference. It would even be a bad sign either for our spirit of asceticism or for our human authenticity, vitality, and strength, if there seemed to be nothing more to obedience than regulated mediocrity, a life without sensations or excitement, a smooth, comfortable, bureaucratic existence. We would be doing our duty and receiving our food in return, we would be contented and therefore would not make any great claims on life. This is not what religious obedience really means. It is really the sacrifice of a value of central importance as an act of faith.

2. *Obedience in the service of the church*

Our religious obedience has of course another aspect: the ecclesial and apostolic aspect. This obedience, of a world-denying, ascetic character, as a mysterious, almost incomprehensible sacrifice of faith, is also placed at the service of ecclesial objectives. Firstly, at the service of the community life; secondly, at the service of the church's apostolate. It is as a result of these things that religious obedience and ecclesial obedience to superiors in the church acquire a new, additional meaning which has a positive value and is important for its own sake, which can sustain and justify religious obedience, not indeed as a whole, but still to a large extent.

A religious order placed at the service of the apostolate has a common task. A common work, a common external aim, needs a structuring, a unification, a general orientation of effort, and from this aspect too needs obedience. Thus ascetic obedience acquires a very practical purpose and meaning. This involves the danger of mistaking and overlooking the ultimate, religious, ascetic, even mystical aspect of faith. Obedience can retain the most essential supernaturally ascetic meaning, even when religious superiors or other authorities in the church issue orders which seem very problematic, perhaps very stupid, very wrong, very old-fashioned in relation to the apostolic purpose of obedience. It is obvious however that obedience does not cease to have meaning or justification when this apostolic objective is not attained. This of course does not mean that every order of a superior is as such always legitimate.

3. *Authority and obedience*

A third point that we must consider is authority and obedience in the pluralism of reality and of the christian virtues. What does this mean? We have already observed that even the radical renunciation involved in the evangelical counsels is not intended as an absolute, physical sacrifice of the values represented there (leaving aside for the time being the question of marriage and celibacy). In any case, it is possible to want to be absolutely poor in a material sense without actually being poor. Nevertheless, in this respect too, by comparison with the attitude of the lay christian, it can be a question only of a different emphasis, important quantitatively, but not of an ultimately essential difference. The layman too must renounce things which represent positive values for him, at least when God does actually take them away.

On the other hand, the religious cannot possibly live only on asceticism. A life wholly dominated by this asceticism as renunciation and sacrifice of human values would not be christian, but perhaps buddhist. If the christian wanted to turn renunciation into a single-minded attitude, monopolising all his life, he would be denying in practice, if not in theory, the reality of the human values which are not pure grace; these values would not be brought into the consummation of the kingdom of God. Both attitudes would be heretical, for ultimately the perfection of man and of the christian consists in the absolute and final salvation of christian and human realities by the supreme values of divine grace, of uncreated grace, down to the transfiguration of the body.

The attitude of the christian, also of the christian who is a religious, must imply always and everywhere the ultimate affirmation of God as God of nature and supernature in regard to all created things. That is why *a priori*, renunciation as such can never be absolute. This holds too for obedience.

Obedience cannot exist without an autonomous disposal by the individual of his freedom. Obedience and authority are very important factors in the life of the religious, which he must respect; but they could never completely guide his life. Even the religious who would leave it to his superior to approve, confirm, direct and guide the smallest details of his life, still cannot avoid putting some suggestions before the superior. Even if he declares that he will leave everything to the absolute discretion of the superior and thus allow himself to be treated "like a stick in the hand of an old man" or "like a corpse", he is by that very fact making an autonomous gesture which he could not have left to the superior to initiate.

Simply because I am free – and obedience itself is dependent on this – I must necessarily have autonomous impulses which cannot be ruled by the superior. Heaven does not first ask the superior what inspirations and impulses to bestow on the individual. The situation has changed then, even for the superior, before questions are asked. He can then always still give directions, he can choose; but he directs what has already begun, his choice has already been made by someone else. It is only as one factor in a plurality of impulses, dynamisms, that he tries to see something of what he can do about projects put before him and submitted to his authority. This does not mean merely that obedience is kept within proper and reasonable limits, which all ascetic tirades cannot set aside, but that a very considerable responsibility is imposed on us.

In other words, I can never say that everything is in the best of order because the superior has given his blessing. I have to recognise that, in spite of my obedience, I have an absolute responsibility before God which neither superiors nor obedience can take away from me. This is a truism, but you would not think so when you read the normal ascetic effusions on obedience. They overlook this fact, but they do not thereby encourage obedience: they make asceticism too cheap. For this renunciation of my freedom, of my autonomous responsibility, even with the best will in the world on the part of the most punctilious superiors and on the part of the most obliging subjects, can in fact only go part of the way. It cannot go further, since the superior cannot have merely *materia prima* to deal with in the subject, but is facing another person, someone with charisms, with the autonomous impulses of his freedom.

If authority and obedience constitute one element in a greater reality and in a pluralism of the christian virtues, obedience cannot be made to bear the whole burden of a man's spiritual life and way of life, of decisions and guidance. Superiors cannot want this, even if they sometimes behave as if they preferred subjects so completely obedient.

Here again it is clear that this pluralism is in a sense incalculable. How far I may permit myself to be influenced by the superior, how far I am active myself, when I make my own plans and when I take over what others have planned: all these things must remain within the framework of obedience. When the superior says, "Thus far and no farther", he is right and his "No" will be respected. But the possibility remains of adding larger or smaller doses of obedience and no one can deprive me of the right to make my own estimate of the dosage.

St Ignatius does in fact say here and there that we must fulfil every wish of the superior. But he is not all that serious about it: in practice, he shows that he has no great opinion of subjects who do this. Within the framework of obedience, I must do things which are not at all to the liking of the superior. If he simply will not have this, he should have the guts and the manliness to accept his responsibility and say: "That must stop!" But in pastoral practice, in education, in scholarship, you cannot adapt yourself one hundred per cent to just any arbitrary wishes, opinions, attitudes or tastes of the superior. This would be impossible if only because you cannot in the last resort jump out of your skin, and because a superior may not always be particularly sympathetic to you.

Obviously we can assume that our superiors never order anything which they consider subjectively to be a sin. But we must certainly allow for the possibility of superiors ordering something that is objectively against the commandment of Christ and the church and of moral theology: something that is objectively impossible for the subject, but is not perceived to be such by the superior. In such a case, a person must really have the courage to appeal to his conscience and refuse to obey the commandment. This does not often occur, but its rarity may perhaps be due to the fact that we are too lax. But if anyone were to think that these simple and obvious facts justified him in grumbling, protesting, muttering about his conscience whenever something was not to his taste, he would be wrong. We cannot hope to avoid such wrong conclusions if we simply pigeon-hole the correct principles, suppressing them without openly denying them.

4. *Practical conclusions*

There must be a real will to obedience as an act of selflessness in faith: the will and desire to experience in this life an absolute test of faith. Why should we not want at some time to face a situation in which we are really obeying without being praised by superiors, without being recognised by men, because we seek nothing but God and because by the very fact of exercising our freedom we are surrendering ourselves to God?

Moreover, it is a part of true obedience to take the initiative and make our own decisions in the line of duty. We have not only the right, but today more than ever the duty, to take the initiative. Our apostolic situation particularly presents so many facets today, is so complicated, so far beyond the supervision of the individual superior, that a religious order would be a boring, dismal set of people unless its subjects also developed a large measure of initiative. However intelligent the superior may be, he cannot really understand something about all the modern opportunities for the apostolate. If he is intelligent and does not think he knows something about everything, he can lead his subjects only in a very formal sense; he can often in a way say no more than: "Think this over sensibly and, if you decide you must act differently, then do so. You also have my blessing for it." Thus each takes on and has to bear a large measure of responsibility.

There is also a responsibility of our own, of which no one can deprive us, even if something is quite clearly ordered; for then too we can at least be asked if we have seriously and honestly tried to discover whether sin is involved or not. This much is not only our right, but our duty. We can certainly assume that what is ordered is morally unobjectionable. But we can have no more than a presumption. We are never dispensed from the responsibility of forming our conscience in regard to what is ordered.

Real obedience includes the courage to be a troublesome subject. Not a grumbler, not one who is always complaining, who always knows better, who cannot fit in anywhere, who presumes *a priori* that whatever the superiors order is absurd and unreasonable until the contrary is proved. There are subjects like this and to some extent we have all been among them. If an unsympathetic superior orders us to do something, we are very easily inclined – and this is understandable – to look first for reasons for saying that it is absurd, instead of trying at once to understand its meaning. But all this does not alter the fact that we must have the courage to be troublesome subjects.

And, independently of the question whether a definite obligation is imposed, we should also have the will and strive constantly to be amiable, friendly, agreeable subjects, meeting our superiors too in a proper, manly and refined manner. This too belongs to the marginal, human phenomena of a religious obedience.

13 THE PRIEST AND MEN

The priest has a unique relationship with men. As the epistle to the Hebrews says (5:1), he is "appointed on behalf of men": his whole being is dedicated to the service of others. He does not exist for himself: he has a function which orientates him with his whole life, his talk, his action, his example, his sacrifice and suffering, to other human beings. He is an apostle – just that, sent to serve.

1. *Love and mission*

This orientation of the priest and his priesthood to other people is sustained by his christian and universal love of neighbour; it is in a true and genuine sense a fulfilment of this christian love of neighbour. Human beings, by their very nature, are always essentially related to one another. This orientation of men to one another develops and is articulated in different ways according to the diverse strata of human nature. They live in one and the same physical world; through their mutual consanguinity they belong to a special type in the biological world; they are related to one another through the exchange of objective intellectual goods and values, of truth, of goodness. They are ultimately related to each other as person to person and finally united with one another by one and the same Holy Spirit, who elevates, sanctifies and raises up into the life of God all these underlying human strata and the mutual relationships in which they are involved.

In possession of the one Holy Spirit of God and the participation in the divine life that this gives, they are united with one another and related to one another in an intimacy that cannot be surpassed, since they can make God's Holy Spirit the unitive factor between them. Thus a community is created: a community based on mutual exchange of saving, redeeming and deifying truth and on mutual benevolence which can touch the salvation – that is, the deepest core – of the other person; and a community of inexchangeable individual persons. This is and remains obviously the supernatural foundation sustaining the priestly relationship to the other person.

If it is true that the priest genuinely possesses and fulfils his priestly nature only when he personally believes, hopes, loves, is justified and holy, then his relationship to the other person must as such be sustained by that infused, divine virtue of supernatural love in the Holy Spirit which justifies man and places him in an intimate relationship to God himself and his neighbour. This neighbour is really and truly loved in and with God, for God's sake and in the light of God, and can be loved deeply and intimately only through the supernatural deifying power of the Holy Spirit whom God has given to us in the supernatural life of grace. All official mandates and official equipment must be ontologically and existentially of lesser consequence than that divine self-communication which consists in justifying grace: just because it is ultimately the uncreated self-communication of God to justified man, nothing can be greater or more important than this grace. Hence it is clear that all official priestly relations to men can be based only on this supernatural love of men, no matter how important are the special mandates involved.

It follows that, whenever the priest fails to realise in his priestly calling this most radical relationship to his fellow man which exists in God himself and in his divine life, he will also fail to come up to the requirements of his work as a priest. It follows likewise that all inner vitality, closeness, personal esteem for the other person must be included in the "heart to heart" of christian love of neighbour. Face the fact that you are properly a priest only if you truly love your neighbour as God in his Holy Spirit gives men power to love.

This priestly relationship to our neighbour should be sustained by supernatural love and, up to a point, represents a quite specific fulfilment of this love. The priest in his mission formally and explicitly wills his neighbour's salvation, his supernatural union with God, and thus expresses and makes official the inner core of love of neighbour, which is to love him in as much as he is loved by God. From this standpoint too we see how the merely authoritative, official, institutional factor not only does not define and cannot constitute by itself the relationship of the priest to men, but that this real, warm, vital, selfless, genuine love for the other person as such belongs to the priestly relationship to men.

2. *Humble authority*

Of course, the priest's relationship – in as much as he is a priest to the other person, even if it is not something higher than other relationships – is certainly something special. For there is an important, if perhaps supplementary factor underlying this relationship ontologically, supernaturally, ethically, which constitutes in the priesthood a special mission and thus a specific relationship to our neighbour. "We are ambassadors for Christ", says St Paul (2 Cor 5:20).

We are apostles, commissioned, sent on an official, authoritative mission to men. This gives a specific character to our universal christian love in which we really want the salvation of the other person. This ministering function is an authoritative function: the priest acts in the name of God. He is present as God's envoy. He proclaims God's word, not his own; it is God's grace he administers, not men's.

When we thus rightly claim God's authority before the people to whom we are sent, we must never forget that this authority is to be realised only in faith on both sides; otherwise it cannot be really present at all. For that reason, it is not to be compared with other authorities known to men, personal or otherwise; and it is just this that must also be seen in the way in which the claim to priestly authority in regard to men is asserted. People must see that this messenger himself is committed and sent in a conscience enlightened by faith and does not come to men as one wielding power and full of his own importance. The person who feels this authoritative function of the priest as directed at himself must be able to observe how this assertion of authority humbles the priest, makes him more unassuming, and seems to him more of a burden than anything else, since he perceives his own inadequacy as a bearer of this divine mandate.

It is a question of an authority over men different from any other that we know. The identity between the claim to authority and the holder of this authority is not the same in the priest as it is in the learned person in regard to the unlearned, the father in regard to the infant, political authority in regard to its subjects. This must be made clear in our behaviour towards other men. There must be no more of what is regarded as clerical arrogance, clerical self-confidence, clerical lust for power, which still exists even today. But today priestly authority can no longer be linked with greater learning as in the middle ages or with the colour of our skin as missionaries to savages. In former times this sort of thing was perhaps inevitable. The medieval priest simply could not avoid making the distinction that he could read and write while Charlemagne could not. Vestiges of this way of thinking continue to influence us even today, but it is just this odd sort of mix-up that we must avoid. We are not more clever, better educated, not necessarily more mature, nor does the very fact of being priests make us more holy, but we have to invoke an authority which humbles us in regard to other men.

3. *An important, but not the sole function*

This priestly function in regard to other men is one particular function and relationship within the totality of human functions, dimensions and relationships. At some point every man is tempted to assert his own self-confidence – which in a sense is necessary for his existence – by claiming an absolute importance for himself and his task, at least in the circle which at all interests him. This tendency exists also among the clergy. This is always a danger for ourselves, and in fact in two ways: either we exaggerate our importance and minimise that of all other men or we become uncertain of the value of our priestly life: we feel that we are out-manoeuvred and not really taken seriously. Both attitudes are wrong.

We must quite calmly recognise that the priest too is a player, an important player, in the great drama that God produces in world history and in which he himself takes part in his eternal Word, the Word made man. But this is not to say that he is unique, just because from one particular aspect he plays a decisive role; it does not mean that all others are insignificant, that all other functions depend on us. We must strive to gain the humility, the courage, the inner self-assurance, to feel that we are God's envoys and to allow other people to live in a different way.

The priest must see things without prejudice: he is sent by God; he must fulfil his function within the totality of human life and human history. He need not feel threatened in his self-consciousness, self-confidence and self-respect, if there are things in science which he does not understand, if he is not up to date in matters of art, if he is not just the right person in other human relationships and dimensions.

This priestly function – and this is precisely what constitutes its closest relationship to christian love of neighbour – is ultimately one which is related to the individual as such. In the last resort, priests don't exist for the church, but for men's salvation. But this salvation of men must always be established through the freedom of the individual person. Of course the priest has ecclesiastical functions, which are related to the church as community, but these too are themselves directed to the salvation of the individual. He has to bear witness to christianity and the grace of God, and thus clearly show that priesthood, church and so on have nothing to do with a power-complex in society.

The conception of the priestly function as one of ministry to the individual human being in his individual salvation is more than ever necessary today. It is of course also a function which, even though sustained by christian love of neighbour, is not always for that reason accepted joyously and gratefully. There is really the "in season and out of season" (2 Tim 4:2) in the priest's relationship to his neighbour. The priest must also bear witness to his neighbour of God's truth, which can be painful, and of God's law, which can be hard. He must also stand up for the rights of God, even though these rights of God, which he claims, are ultimately nothing more than the right of love in which God wills to give himself as infinite bliss to men and claims no other right but to love man and with this love of his to be accepted by man. But for someone who is still immature as a human being and a christian, this right of God, which a priest must defend, may seem hard. Even then the priest has to exercise this function.

4. *The priest and particular classes of men*

Every priest has a certain affinity to particular types of men. He should easily make contact with these, but as priest he must also be accessible to men generally. Every priest therefore should meet men quite boldly, but at the same time without putting on airs. Take a look at the particular classes of men whom you will meet as a priest and ask yourself: How far am I succeeding in establishing an inner relationship with very young children, schoolchildren and students, with narrow-minded, pious people who are also and must be allowed in the kingdom of God, with university people, with the proletariat, with dubious characters, with those on the fringe of the church, with artists, with the sick and the dying? If we look at our practical behaviour as priests, we shall certainly see that our personal affinity for certain classes of men means that we have little time left over for the rest. We then tend to avoid other priestly tasks. And perhaps we over-estimate the work that we do as a result of our inner affinity for one group of people. We may perhaps be unfair to priests who have a special pastoral relationship with other people.

5. *The priest and woman*

After speaking of the priest's relationship with different classes of people, this would seem to be the place to consider expressly the priest's relationship to woman. You are old enough to know the importance, the difficulty, the burden, the arduousness of celibacy. In the Latin church you took on this obligation of celibacy as subdeacons. There is scope for a good deal of thought on the question of celibacy in the light of the principles of pastoral theology and also on its suitability in one respect or another. Why should we expect to be able to realise all our human possibilities in any one form of life, just because it is good and holy? A doctor cannot realise in his life just that fullness of life which a musician realises. He seizes on *one* value and – in this finite life, in this finite time, with finite resources, with finite human possibilities – necessarily renounces others. This holds too if we reach out for the value, for the evangelical way of life, represented by celibacy. This we must calmly and clearly affirm, in order then to live in absolute fidelity in accordance with our acceptance of this way of life.

There is of course very much more that could be said on this subject. Celibacy should not be made the centre of the priestly life, as if it were the most important thing in our life. It is not the easiest or the most obvious thing. It is a great and important task, a hard task, even though not the most central in our life, genuinely and completely to make this renunciation, to make it in such a way that nothing will be destroyed or left un-cultivated which is not compensated by the spiritual power, the divine love, resulting from this way of life. Even if, strictly in terms of moral theology, celibacy is achieved without sin, it creates genuinely human dangers which can and must be avoided. There is the danger of becoming desiccated; of lapsing – as Clement of Alexandria said long ago – in a sublime, but only too real way into misanthropy through celibacy; of not escaping altogether unscathed as a result of attaching too much importance to comfort, repose, an easy con-science. These dangers must be avoided.

Ultimately, this is possible only if we keep alive the positive ideals of our calling, if we have intellectual interests, if we work hard, if we have a healthy ambi-tion and a healthy desire to achieve something, if we cultivate a life of prayer and enter as closely as possible into a personal union with God. Finally there must be a firm will to renunciation, and pedagogic and psy-chological prudence in regard to ourselves, so that all these things are not made more difficult than they really are: in other words, to live intelligently the life we have chosen and to shoulder the burden freely and gladly accepted out of love for Jesus Christ and for souls, in such a way that it absorbs no more strength than is necessary for coming to terms with this task. If we have no more spiritual force left over, because we are sitting – so to speak – on the powder barrel of our sexuality and have to use all our force on preventing an explosion, then we have certainly misunderstood and realised in the wrong way the celibacy that God offered us as his true grace.

The priest has to deal with human beings and when he really loves these human beings in a priestly spirit, in labour and sacrifice, he has really fulfilled his christianity and his own proper destiny. For it is true that the law is summed up in the one commandment of love of neighbour (Mt 22:39) and the person who selflessly finds his neighbour has also found God.

14 THE PRIEST OF TODAY

This meditation on the priesthood is not meant so much to describe the essential theological features of the priesthood as to follow up the question of what a priest of today ought to look like, what characteristics modern man expects to find or particularly misses in the priest. Of course the model set before us makes excessive demands. It is part of the essence of the priestly calling that it requires of a man more than he can accomplish from his own resources, just as loving God with all one's heart and all one's strength (Mt 22:37) always overburdens the person at some point, since he can never say that he has satisfied the claim made upon him; just as christianity generally in the sermon on the mount (Mt 5:1f), in the commandment of love (Mk 12:28–31), in the commandment to imitate the crucified (Mt 16:24–26), always calls man out, forces him out, into an infinity which he cannot master by his own power, in regard to which he always remains the beginner, the one who falls short of the demand. This too is how we feel about the priesthood. It lies in the nature of the case.

1. *Individual apostle in the mass-age*

The priest of today is in a special degree the individual apostle in the age of the masses. Of course the church – as she was known in church history – is the great church, she wants to be a church of the people and of the masses. She baptises young children impartially, counts them as her own, expects the masses of the baptised to stay with her, to be and to become catholic christians. The church will never abandon in principle the idea of being in this sense a church of the masses, a people's church.

You are aware that this catchword has roused violent controversy in our time both within the catholic church in Central Europe and outside catholic christianity. We are told that a person becomes a christian, he is not born so: hence the whole orientation of pastoral care to large "flocks" is wrong and anyway can no longer be maintained today. This is not what we are trying to say here. Nevertheless, it is a fact that christians today are a relatively small flock in a large mass. If we recall the fact that, in Germany for instance, there are at least 50 per cent of christians who are not catholic and that out of the remaining 50 per cent, no more than 10–30 per cent are practising, it is easy to see how few real christians there are. Certainly the church remains then a small flock, a more or less poverty-stricken lot.

This is the situation in which we have to work as priests. Even if we are a church of the people and of the masses, if we try to hold on to all the positions we have inherited historically, if we defend the official christian façade of a culture and a civilisation which fulfils less than it promises, it still remains true that our task is to fight for each individual person, to try to make him a christian within this situation, a person who still believes cheerfully, in spite of this liberal, atheistic, sceptical milieu. That is why our priestly action must be directed to making something quite splendid and wonderful out of every non-christian who becomes a christian, a success for which we can never sufficiently thank God.

It is to be hoped that we have the courage to esteem highly the individual in his christianity, so that a person who becomes a christian appears as a reward, as a blessing for our priestly life. This attitude is part of the priestly ethos; it is something we need if we are not always to have the impression of struggling strenuously but vainly against an irresistible, progressive dechristianisation. The priest will always be the shepherd of a flock and always head of a community, but this does not mean that the community has to be particularly large. Consequently, he is the apostle of an individual destiny: the priest is the one who has the courage to be such an apostle.

2. *Mystagogue of a personal piety*

From the standpoint of salvation-history, this age of the masses cannot be regarded as bearing the official imprint of christianity: the priest now, much more than formerly, must be the mystagogue of a personal piety. What is properly spiritual, by contrast with mere administration in the purely sacramental and institutionally social sphere, has certainly gained a new importance today in the priest's life. He cannot simply feed the flock and let the individual take his chance with them. This happens to an ever decreasing extent.

In the confessional, in personal discussion, the priest today more than ever must work for a personal piety of the individual as such. Christianity must have dawned on this christian in a unique, individual fashion as his wholly unexpected grace; he may perhaps be sad that others around him have not apparently shared in this grace, but his inner life as a christian must be such that the absence of christianity in his neighbourhood does not appear as a threat. At the same time, the priest is the mediator, the man who initiates people into a wholly personal piety. From all this it is obvious that today in our own priestly life we can be less than ever religious officials, ecclesiastical functionaries of an ecclesiastical undertaking.

3. Truly human

Such a priest today must be utterly and genuinely human. He must be able to win people, to meet them as man to man. He must make some effort to be convincing also when as an individual he comes up against the critical attitude of another person. He cannot always simply feel that the armies of God and the church are behind him, that he is the great herald of the church of the masses, 300 or 500 million strong, ready to sound the trumpet and cry: "Here we come!" In our non-christian mass-age he will not get at people in this way. Small and insignificant, he comes before the individual and can effectively win over the other person only by showing in the light of his own christianity that it is worth while to be a christian. In this situation he must be convincing also as a human being.

Seen correctly in terms of dogmatic theology, man's natural-moral behaviour is not something that fails to bear witness to grace, not something purely secular, having practically nothing at all to do with christianity. If in the dogmatic theology of grace we say that in the long run the natural law can be observed only with the grace of Christ – whether men know that it is the grace of Christ or not, is irrelevant – this means that the genuine, mature, pure, modest, joyous human reality is itself a testimony to the fact that Christ's grace is in the world. This at any rate is what modern man expects. Saints who seem to reach the point at which they are stunted, humanly speaking, may perhaps be very holy, but their realisation of this laudable holiness in their lives is not very effective for the apostolate. To be human in a christian way does not simply mean to be "conformed to this world" (Rom 12:2), but implies that the person who meets us has the chance to see that being a christian is not something contrary to his basic feelings.

The priest of today must be truly human in this sense. He must have the courage to believe also in the God-given, "natural" nature in himself – for all the self-criticism he has learnt to apply in the light of the doctrines of concupiscence and original sin, of the danger of evil, of the devil and the world. It is possible to combine these things. We don't need to think that christian asceticism succeeded at all times in achieving a synthesis between a true confidence in God's creative power and confidence in human goodness; nor do we need to consider all the teachings of the older asceticism as appropriate and valid in every respect for the present time.

The priest of today must be somehow educated in a broader sense without on that account pretending to be expert in everything. People expect the priest to be an educated man. Since we took our final examinations, studied philosophy and theology, we have acquired a certain amount of education, but it is not this that people expect of us today. Our education must be more human, more general, must be linked with an interest for just those things which interest modern man. Obviously we don't need to know everything. We cannot be atomic physicists, psychologists, paleontologists, sociologists, literary experts and politicians in our spare time. But it would sometimes be more reasonable to read a newspaper or to settle down with a novel than to play cards. We really have a duty to be genuine, educated human beings. This means also that our education must not be merely intellectual, but an inner formation of the whole man – including his emotions.

4. *Fraternal companions under the burden of faith*

Without being affected or sentimental, indiscreet or lacking in respect, the priest today is expected to feel in a special way that he is a fraternal companion sharing the other person's burden of faith. Even if someone feels the burdens and darkness of faith really, bitterly, almost as threatening his existence, there is still a genuine, spontaneous and firm faith. The absolute peak of faith or – in theological terms – the most radical fullness of the infused virtue of faith is quite compatible with faith's darkness, its toilsomeness, the feeling of being constantly under attack.

There are those who take their faith for granted, who regard those who don't or think they don't believe as either knaves or fools. For these, firm faith is not grace-given, supernaturally infused faith in itself, but is rather a product of sociological conditions, of psychological fixation of an attitude. For the most part, this kind of firmness has not very much to do with true firmness of faith.

It is of course clear that God's grace and his guidance, building on our peculiarities, our personal history, our environment, gives us a faith undisturbed by threats, joyous, secure. If this is our state, we should simply thank God for it, be happy and see that the faith we have thus been given grows abundantly and produces fruit in our priestly life. We don't have to invent ways of increasing the troubles and burden of faith. But if our christian experience is very different, we should not deprive ourselves of the radical certainty of faith, based on the grace of God and the ultimate fidelity of man's freedom.

When this is our experience, we should find in our approach as priests to others that just through this burden of grace, of faith, which God lays upon us we have a new and positive chance of understanding man today. We can give him this message of faith in such a way that a troubled atheist, who has become almost schizophrenic through the plurality of modern sciences, through the discrepancies of method, who scarcely knows any longer how he can combine his other intellectual attitudes with this peculiar attitude of faith, receives from us what no one else can give. When we can do this, we may and should have the courage to be the fraternal companion of the other person in the burden of the darkness, the hardship, the assailability of his faith.

5. *Credibility through honesty*

It is also true that the priest of today will be convincing if he frankly admits his incapacity and the limits of his knowledge. Just take a look at yourselves. At some point, the priest is the one who is certain, superior, who

153

knows all the important things, has a clear, decided philosophy of life, and is tempted to pose as beyond criticism.

What is the true state of affairs? To put it pointedly and paradoxically, christianity is not the religion which solves all the riddles of the universe, but that which gives man courage in the grace of God to shelter himself and his life in an incomprehensible mystery and to believe that this mystery is love. We don't master death, suffering, pain, futility, poverty, sickness, the immense abundance of reality which threatens to overwhelm man's mental powers, by saying that God is the solution to all riddles. This is in fact true, but it has to be understood in the sense that we place this final, all-embracing mystery where it belongs. This God of ours is the incomprehensible, the mystery, and not someone to hide behind; he is therefore not a point from which we could see through and in this sense master completely the rest of reality.

Modern man knows all this and feels it too keenly to be able to put up with a priest acting as if he were God's overseer, as if he had been present at the heavenly council, as if up to a point he could take to pieces the machinery of world-history and explain it to everybody, someone who has a ready solution for all man's queries and torments. In the last resort, all that we can say to people is: Kneel down with me, pray to the incomprehensible God and believe that he is eternal love. As such, he has given testimony of himself in the darkness of the world in Jesus Christ, the crucified. If we raise up over our life someone nailed to a cross, if we understand a little of what this is supposed to mean and if our sense of the enormity of such a symbol is not entirely blunted, then as priests also we must be able to say that we know nothing, we are aware of our limits, we are bearing the cross. We kneel before the incomprehensible mystery of God. We fall down before the God who made us. We can then say that we do really believe "in hope against hope" (Rom 4:18), that we are God's infinitely beloved children.

It is typical of course of this fraternal participation in the other person's burden of faith that we do not act as if we knew everything just because we are educated. We must recognise that we can proclaim christianity only through dialogue. In a certain town in Germany there is a catholic academy. When a new archbishop came, he explained to its director: "My dear man, the academy is all right. I have nothing against it. Keep going. But get this straight: we, the church, the bishops, the priests, really can't discuss things with the people. Discussion is a pedagogic trick and nothing more. We know what we have to say. The others have to listen to it."

This statement is not entirely wrong. We have to convey God's truth and not our own clever inventions. But until God's truth is seized by man and made a reality in his life, it must form part of a synthesis together with the problematical situation and all the unsolved queries of man in general and modern man in particular. And here then are a thousand concrete issues which no one can explain precisely to the priest, which the church too cannot precisely explain to us, on which none of the principles of natural law or other principles, however clear, can throw much light. If the American president were to ask a catholic moral theologian what to do about the atom bomb, what

could the theologian say? What could he do to solve
the final agonies of conscience, the ultimate questions
facing the politician? Nothing! All official principles
are important, splendid, glorious; they must be observed, they are a grace of God; without them the
world would be still darker. But this does not in any
way alter the fact that, even with this light, when it is a
question of God's truth, in the concrete, man is groping
in the dark, arduously making his way through life,
and must try everything possible, not knowing the out-
come. Modern man knows this. If we give the impression that we have no understanding of this situation,
that we know everything, that the gospel has removed
all life's burdens, that we are aware of everything in
all sectors of human knowledge, in all experience of
life, then we make ourselves incredible from the very
outset.

6. *A loving person*

The priest to a very large extent must be one who
loves, who is not self-seeking. This is a truism. But the
priest today, without prejudice to his official, mandatory powers, can exercise his calling only when the
human being is evident, when he is humanly credible,
when he brings in his personal faith in the right way: he
must therefore be someone who is seen by the other
person as a loving, a selfless, a good man. This is easy
to say and we are all ready to answer: "Yes, that's
me". But how shocking, how terrible, is the claim laid
upon us in our priestly life? We once decided how
much duty required and now it seems to be so much
more than we are able to give. We must constantly ask
ourselves: Is our heart, our love, really in our work? If

not, then even in our priesthood we are and remain "noisy gongs, clanging cymbals" (1 Cor 13:1). Hence it is clear that the priest must be the fellow-bearer of the suffering of others.

The world of today banishes suffering into anonymity, renders it inarticulate. We die in hospital so that people don't notice. We must not upset those around us with our suffering. Outwardly, optimism reigns everywhere; and yet inwardly people are in fear, threatened, insecure, suffering, groping in darkness, dreading death, unhappy, and they have developed an almost pathological feeling perhaps in regard to marriage, their profession, their relationship to their children, to the rest of their surroundings, to their own bodily nature, a keen sensitivity to pain. There should be someone to help the other person at this point by sharing the burden, listening to him, being patient with him. It is hard, particularly if we ourselves are vigorous, healthy, successful, enjoying life, to be patient with those who are suffering, whose lot is very different from ours; it is difficult to avoid getting rid of these people quickly, regarding them simply as hysterical, stupid, naive or sentimental. Really to share the burden here, to listen, to get interested, to let people say the same things a thousand times, to put up with their whining, this is a great natural gift and at the same time a gift of grace. There must be someone in the world who takes all this on himself, patiently, while being hard with himself, at least in certain particular cases. The priest must be fellow-bearer of suffering.

7. *Looking for a new language*

The priest must be a fearless seeker after a new

language. Christianity is always the same, the oldest and most obvious, and at the same time can be the utterly new. But it cannot be denied that the language in which we proclaim christianity is often very old-fashioned (not in a literary, aesthetic sense, but in the sense that language exists to bring home reality in the form in which it can best be assimilated). To complain about this no more makes sense than to have fashionable ideas, to attempt cheap tricks. Instead of this, we should question ourselves, should face our own difficulties in all matters of faith without prejudice, fearlessly, guilelessly, and not dodge or pass over these problems, but try to solve them to some extent for ourselves and in ourselves and then tell people the results.

Even then we shall continue to talk in a way that could be improved, but we have perhaps made that small, quite modest contribution which anyone might make. But let us make an effort not to continue handing out the old clichés simply because they are correct, perhaps because they are even in scripture, even used in the church's proclamation up to the present time, in encyclicals too and bishops' pastorals. Don't let us be satisfied with this, but let us try to deliver the gospel of Jesus Christ so that it really does penetrate to some extent into our own heart. Then perhaps there will be others too who hear it.

8. *One who can let other minds count in the church*

The priest of today must have sufficient love to allow other minds to count in the church. The world today is so manifold, so differentiated, so plural, that in the one catholic (that is, all-embracing) church, according to the positive and not merely permissive will of God, there must necessarily be very great differences: in law, in worship, in theology, in pastoral activity, in asceticism, in practical life, the shaping of christianity, in the confrontation of christianity with the world. If we are not broad-minded and tolerant here, if we don't allow things to count in the church which we don't do ourselves, because we cannot do them, because we have no time for them, because we have other gifts of God's grace and not these: if we don't manage this, we are not priests – that is, not priests as we ought to be today.

This professional jealousy, this assumption – for example – that whatever is good is in our own order or is at least borrowed from this if it exists elsewhere, is stupid and naive, untrue, shows a lack of love, is false, even from the ecclesiological standpoint. This however does not mean that we ourselves must run after everything and take everything into our own "shop". We don't have to be a shop where simply everything that is in the church can be bought. Why? An intelligent, mature person can be aware of his own special gifts, however limited. In humility, modesty and patience, he can show his awareness in a completely loving way and without feelings of inferiority, and nevertheless admit that others may have other gifts, great gifts, which are necessary to the church. If we cannot be happy in this way with what is our own, even though others have other gifts, then we are not priests of the calibre required in the church today.

9. *Concentration on essentials*

The modern priest must be concerned with essentials in religion. The decisions of faith today, when all faith must be freshly gained, decided, suffered, begged, are necessarily directed to ultimate, essential things in such a way that we have not only the right, but also the duty, in our pastoral work and our asceticism, largely to restrict ourselves to the bare essentials and to leave aside much by way of trimmings and fuss that seemed appropriate in former times. Consider the new churches, how little there is in them of furnishing and adornment by comparison with former times. This is not the result of chance. We have so much to do with the ultimate, basic things that we cannot keep hundreds of different devotions going, however beautiful and good they may be.

The priest therefore should not bother people today with any sort of irrelevancy; he should really preach what is essential and decisive. I have nothing against devotion to our Lady of Fatima, but if our hearts are gladdened and our religious humanity awakens only when we preach something of this kind, we must pull ourselves up and realise that we have to speak of Jesus Christ, of the eucharist, of God, of his mystery, of the Trinity. This is the point at which the heart of the truly religious man must be made glad. These are the things, the solid food, which are necessary in pastoral work today.

10. *A discreet man of religion*

The priest today ought to be discreet, unobtrusive, as a man of religion. If we talk pompously and noisily about God, if we are not discreet, if we do not suffer from a sense of inadequacy when we try to talk about things so great, if we don't therefore talk softly, then we are lacking in a proper reserve, in essential modesty, and as priests we shall fail to be convincing to modern man. It is obvious that the priest today must be a devout man in the most genuine, the truest, the most direct sense.

What we have to give men is faith, hope and love. Everything else they will find at least as easily in other men; they don't need to get it from us. Consequently, modern man looks for a truly religious person, one who has obtained grace from God and seeks it afresh each day in order to commit his life, his whole existence, to real piety, to his relationship with God, although he is quite aware that others neither can nor will do so, nor in fact are doing so, in this radical, professional sense. This specialisation, this concentration on the highest things, is a necessary part of the priestly life. Anyone who thinks that he must do like other men in all other sectors of life is attempting what is impossible in the finiteness of human existence; he inevitably leaves too little scope for what he should be and is therefore unable to give to others what they expect of him and only of him.

11. *A man of ecumenical outlook*
The priest today must acquire, possess and develop an understanding for non-catholic christian denominations, although he remains convinced of the absolute claim of the one Roman catholic church. This attitude is not yet present in the church to the extent it should be.

12. *A true non-conformist*
The priest is expected to have the courage to be a non-conformist when the occasion requires it, without

making non-conformity into a principle. When the priest creates the impression that he is simply a minor official, swearing to the party-line when there is really no necessity to do so, when he finds everything wonderful, unsurpassable, that appears in the dullest parish magazine or in any other "catholic" medium of communication, then he becomes incredible. If however he thinks he can avoid this weak and cowardly non-conformism by simply running down everything that is not defined as a truth of faith, he will likewise fail to gain understanding and love for the church and christianity.

13. *A man who speaks freely in the church*

It follows also from all this that the priest should take the risk of speaking freely in the church. This free speech – as Pius XII said – belongs to the church and, without it, "an injury would be done to pastor and flock." This courage too, of course, must not degenerate into ecclesiastical quarrelsomeness.

14. *A happy man*

The priest must be in a good and true sense a happy man. A short time ago, in Freiburg, the mother of a priest was dying. She drank a glass of champagne with her son and then said: "Go home now and sleep well, and I shall sleep into eternity. Don't look too sad about it. If priests look sad, nobody believes what they preach." *Et factum est ita.*

15. *Teacher of freedom*

The priest must be able to train men for freedom, for personal christianity. Those confessors who try to attach everybody to themselves are wrong. And, as we have said, the priest is the one who admits his own embarrassing lack of knowledge and by this very fact wins people for the religion of God and not for his own human cleverness. He does not extol the christian faith as the solution of all the riddles of the universe, but simply understands it as the loving acceptance of mystery.

15 DANGERS FOR THE PRIESTHOOD TODAY

We close our series of meditations on the priesthood with a consideration of the dangers facing the priesthood today.

1. *Love of danger for its own sake*

One danger for the priest today is undoubtedly that of seeking danger for its own sake. Today we cannot go on in every respect living – as the priest in former times could and did – this regulated life, subject to supervision from the first, tried out and classified a thousand times in its practical form. This is not possible: the situation is too complicated, the tasks too varied, the experiences always new. Thus, particularly with the open-minded, the impression easily arises that everything ought to be done differently from the way it has been done hitherto.

This of course is largely false, but not because there is not a great deal that ought to be done in a different way, or because the fact is not to be deplored that a great deal is not done differently for the reason that opposition to such changes is to be expected on the part of ecclesiastical superiors. The idea is false because the truth of Jesus Christ, the divine structure of the church of Jesus Christ, and the experience of two thousand years, undoubtedly outweighs what could and should be done differently, however true it may be that the little which ought to be changed might be of capital importance for the whole success of the apostolic mission of the church. In this respect we cannot and may not underestimate small changes, in fact we cannot esteem them highly enough.

Since there is much that could be different today, much that ought to be freshly thought out, planned and managed, we may easily be inclined to break down, for the sake of breaking down, those ascetic and moral assurances once regarded as covering the danger. Where things like this could happen, we should be a little distrustful of ourselves and draw the appropriate conclusions. A certain caution, a certain reserve, a certain mistrust, on the part of superiors is not to be dismissed *a priori* as old-fashioned philistinism.

There is also the danger today on the one hand of assuming always that the new must be the better or on the other hand of clinging in a sterile conservatism to the old as necessarily final. Each one must examine himself sincerely and self-critically about the danger to which he is more likely to be exposed. If some people are inclined to be passive, why shouldn't they admit this? These could see that revolutionary outbreaks are not the greatest danger into which they might be drawn. They could admit that they are presumably too cautious, too slow, too pedantic, too intent on the letter of the existing law.

For every man has his own peculiarity. In every peculiarity there is something positive and in every peculiarity there is danger. Since we are all sinful men, this danger too will obviously find expression. Anyone who assumes that he will not also have to pay for his own limited peculiarity in an objectively perverse, even sinful way, is deceiving himself, contradicting catholic dogma, and is in any case very naive.

Of course this is a very commonplace and simple matter which everyone will admit theoretically and in the abstract. But we must ask ourselves where the greater danger lies for us, admit that there is a danger in our own mentality, that in view of her God-willed pluralism no one ever has all the right in the church of God, that there was never a time in the history of the church when one side was a hundred per cent right and the other side a hundred per cent false and that this always became clear at a later date. We must work out, see and admit all this intelligently, we must be critical towards ourselves and patient with others, we must be tolerant towards others and yet have the courage to advocate something quite definite and even controversial. We must be resigned to the fact that God may commission us to do one thing and yet likewise wants the other, the opposite side, in the church. For that reason we can love, respect and tolerate, we can have understanding for the other. Then self evident principles will not be quite so impractical as they may seem at first sight.

2. *Impersonal routine*

A further danger consists in the impersonal routine of our priestly life. At some point our priestly life is defined sociologically and intellectually also by the fact that it must follow a track marked out in advance, that it is controlled by definite norms. This is both useful, necessary and God-willed, and also enormously dangerous for the religious life. Hence there arises the danger of impersonal routine in religious matters: something that the modern man takes very badly indeed, unless he is a good christian from the very beginning.

3. *Ordinariness as a principle*

A further danger which unavoidably exists in such a state of life, but which must be overcome, is to make the ordinary, the average, into a principle. In every state of life there must be a certain average requirement, a certain normality in conduct. Hence it is easy for the parsimonious, the cowardly, the sinner, to think that this average quasi-legally imposed norm is all that must be personally attained and that nothing more is required. The individual makes the average that is legally required into a principle for his personal life. He imagines moreover that this average is the absolute maximum that can be required of him. He is quite intelligent and thinks he has done his duty if he more or less gets through his trials, since he has evidently done what he had to do, for the others too are not required to do more.

This judgment is completely false. For, before God and his conscience, before the church, he has the serious and sacred duty to achieve more than is demanded of him. It is just this greater achievement, which cannot be given legal expression, to which he is bound in conscience, and any adaptation of his personal activity to this dull mediocrity is wrong and reprehensible. In all this the further danger of adopting an official's mentality becomes evident.

4. *Asceticism from despair*

A further danger is that of an asceticism which results from despair and an inferiority complex. There are people who fall at some stage into a gloomy, false asceticism as a means of saving their self-respect. There are men who looked for the wrong thing in the priesthood, something not spiritually clarified, and failed to attain it; then, because they stick to the priesthood by God's grace and in virtue of their decision, they seek a kind of fresh justification in a wrong way in their "No" to the world, in asceticism, in outward observances, and – worse still – they also find it.

It is possible to be a very zealous person, seriously striving after holiness, without giving way to this danger. Whenever someone becomes really soured, when people keep out of his way, when he snoops around as if he were the bad conscience of the others, there is something wrong. There is a malformation of true, religious, priestly striving. Those people should also be seen in this light who take refuge in a very zealous but wasteful activity, are ferociously industrious, but fall short as men of religion. Work, industry, mixing with people, must not be an anaesthetic to deaden the real pain of renunciation which lies at the entry into religious life, so that the real thing is missed, the very thing which should grow in us only through this pain of true renunciation, of loneliness, of prayer.

5. *Intolerance in the service of the church*

A further danger for the priestly life is to take a sociologically and historically conditioned life-style, an emphasis, a prevailing trend, as the sole, legitimate *sentire cum ecclesia*. *Sentire cum ecclesia* just does not mean that any particular individual with his own very subjective attitude may pretend to be the embodiment of the church. It must still be said of the church teacher:

in medio ecclesiae aperuit os suum. As individuals, neither bishops nor pope, nor the whole people, are ever the church. Occasionally, they represent the whole church authoritatively and juridically; but not even in the person of a pope does there exist the fullness of what God wants in his church, of what is authorised, concentrated and assembled in the church.

We have no duty to interpret *sentire cum ecclesia* in such a way that an historically or sociologically conditioned taste or life-style or a particular way of seeing things is simply identified with the mind of the church. Of course we have a right and even a sacred duty to live at peace with the other members of the church.

6. *Dread of the unknown future*

There is further the dread of the unknown, new situations and the fear for the future of the church which then again has its effect either in a wild, revolutionary frame of mind or in a nervous conservatism. This danger, too, we must avoid. If we consider reality in the concrete, it is not easy to follow even such an obvious counsel.

16 THE TWO STANDARDS

The following meditations, known as the meditations on election, are of central importance in life and in the teaching of St Ignatius: they have so great a theological and also human depth that it will certainly do no harm to keep these basic, if somewhat formal meditations constantly before us in the retreat. Of course they have their real meaning only at that point in the retreat where a real choice of any importance has to be made in regard to any aspect of life. But if something as fundamental as this is not impossible and if occasionally in a human life apparently slight decisions can be of central importance, we might conclude that it is always useful to make such meditations even in a situation calling for apparently only slight decisions.

If man's life is freedom, then it is decision and election, and this situation always exists to some extent. Since it very often happens in human life that decisive choices are made in regard to slight matters or are spread more or less diffusely over a whole life-time, but in their end-result come to quite unforeseen final points, an asceticism adapted to such ideas in an Ignatian spirit is always relevant.

1. *The meaning of the meditation on the two standards*

The meditation on the two standards (136–148) corresponds to that on the temptation of Christ in the desert (274) in the series of meditations on the life of Jesus. If we place the meditation on the two standards alongside that on the three classes of men, we might say that the former is oriented to salvation history and sets our election within a theological and indeed redemptive-historical framework, while the latter is expressed more in terms of individual psychology and describes the inner mechanisms of choice.

We know the general meaning of this meditation on the two standards. According to Ignatius, the call of Christ the king should be oriented to the decision of an explicit choice and thus also a particular direction to this call of Christ, which has gone out to us in the kingdom of Christ. The question then gradually emerges: how can the genuine call of Christ be distinguished from a false impulse? What must we look for here? Why, in contrast to the meditation on the kingdom of Christ, does the devil come expressly on the scene here for the first time, so to speak as the quintessence of all anti-God impulses? In this meditation on election it is always a question of the "more", and therefore particularly of the appreciation of the dangers of self-deception and delusion.

However simply and straightforwardly Ignatius describes these "two standards" of the two captains, it is plain that the meditation on this radical dualism is profoundly theological in terms of salvation – and world-history. We might say that this notion of the two standards is found everywhere in the history of religion, that it is a theme running through the whole of christian theology from the beginning of the new testament. Already in the old testament Babylon is seen as the evil city, from which the exiles will return to Jerusalem; in the new, particularly in the Book of Revelation, Babylon as the city of Satan is opposed to the new Jerusalem. The terms continued to be used in christian tradition to describe the fundamental redemptive-historical dualism in the world. Augustine's *civitas terrena* and *civitas Dei* are simply elucidations of what Ignatius says in his own way.

The simplicity – one might almost say, the childishness – of this image must not be permitted therefore to blind us to the grandeur of the conception; and we must not simplify this dualism in the world and its history by identifying too directly certain historical factors in the world with the standard of Lucifer and others with the church. For there is nothing in the world that is purely and simply the radical, absolute embodiment of evil, of what is opposed to God, of satanic power, however much certain phenomena in the world seem to point in that direction.

The church too, as the visible church of sinners, is not simply the representative of the standard of Christ: for even in her the sinful, the anti-God, the non-christian element also exists, although not in such a way that "the gates of hell" (Mt 16:18) could overcome her or that she could cease to be the primal sacrament and presence of God's grace and salvation. What is so original in Ignatius is that he sees both the devil (141) and Christ (144) sending flying squads out into the whole world, sees very clearly with Jesus that in the one field of the world both weeds and wheat (Mt 13:24–30) grow up and cannot easily be separated until the Lord of the harvest comes. With Jesus he sees that on the one threshing floor of the world wheat and chaff are mingled and that therefore the important thing for us is to learn to distinguish in our concrete situation between Christ and his following on the one hand and the devil and his following on the other. If these two factors were represented simply, in absolute purity, and easy to distinguish, all that Ignatius is trying to put before us would have been cleared up and disposed of long ago.

2. *Necessity of decision*

In world-history and in our own history there constantly occurs a dividing of the ways: a decision therefore is unavoidable. This simple fact, clear and obvious as it is, is really always an irritant to man, a constant burden; he will not admit it. He would really always like to unite incompatibles in world-history and in his own history. He is constantly wanting to have everything at once; he doesn't want to seize on anything if it means giving up something else; he would prefer not to make a decision. Yet this is absolutely necessary.

Up to a point, he might rightly have the impression that things could be different, because all that is true, good, beautiful, right, worth striving for, comes from God, because there is really nothing that is not in some way worth striving for. For if a thing is, it is good; and if it is good, it is worth striving for; and if we truly strive and are aware of our striving, we are aware too of the reality for which we are striving: if all this is so, it seems that he is right in thinking that he really need not give up anything (and this is the basic temptation in our life), that he can combine everything, that everything can be united in a higher synthesis which might be realised in this life.

And yet this is not true. Decision is necessary, there must be a real choice, so that we cannot have both at once and therefore must decide. This decision begins in the depth of the heart and has its effect in the world: what we see in the world as antagonistic, to be distinguished in a choice, represents merely the reflex of that inner decision which must be made in the depths of our existence. Ignatius tells us, and even Goethe knew, that in a true sense world-history can be reduced to this decision, to these two standards.

The fact of the dividing of the ways and of decision in world-history and in our own personal history must be faced and accepted in all its radicality, harshness, painfulness. We cannot be priests and a variety of other things, we cannot be religious and still want a variety of other things. There are of course decisions which are imposed on us, but which we will not recognise; and there are decisions which offer us a real choice, where we also seek a synthesis which does not exist. All conflicts, all neuroses, are due at least partly to this fact that a person cannot really choose, cannot decide, wants to produce impossible syntheses which do not exist in this life. Christ came to bring a sword, not peace (Mt 10:34).

3. *Technique of seduction*

The first thing of which Ignatius speaks is this fact of a dividing of the ways in world-history and in our history: the necessity of decision. Secondly he describes the technique of seduction.

Since the world is not God and since everything in the world is ambivalent prior to an intellectual decision which cannot ultimately be separated from the person, there exists the basic possibility of blurring over, of double-meaning, and thus the basic possibility of temptation and seduction. Things in themselves – to be a priest or not to be a priest, to marry or not to marry, and so on – are ambivalent and plastic. They can be manipulated and understood in various ways, taken into the core of personal freedom, and evil can tempt us from the purely objective matter on which freedom is exercised, from its ambivalence. Ignatius now describes more exactly how this happens. In the last resort, the devil turns something which in itself is one possible object of choice into an absolute for the person concerned.

According to Ignatius, there are three steps in this temptation (142). In this triple gradation we must not concentrate too much and too exclusively on riches in terms of money-values. Ignatius says that man rises from wanting to possess to wanting to be noticed and to wanting to be and that it is in this triple gradation that the devil tempts man. He begins with wealth in the sense of what confronts man as his fulfilment, possessions in the widest sense of the term, which include money, marriage, earthly fulfilment, culture, spirit, success, power, all that which is in some way different from man and yet is offered to him as fulfilment of his life in this world, which is not identical with God. From the absolutising quest for wealth understood in this way, which man then identifies with himself, arises the desire to be noticed, a kind of craving behind which there naturally lurks the ultimate fear for life, again rooted in unbelief in a specific sense: namely, the nervous clinging to something we are not and which God is not, but which we still think is absolutely necessary for us.

If at any time you have really had to deal with people who are sinners, you can see that these people absolutise some particular thing, their happiness, their orthodoxy or a wrong that has been done to them. They are ready for everything, but there is one thing they will not recognise as relative, as something they can give up. They want to be at peace with God, but only on this particular condition. Without this, they try to suggest, it won't work. They don't say "I will not", but "I cannot". But this "I cannot" is nothing but the expression of this absolute self-identification with a particular good. These people really think that it would kill them, destroy them at the very roots of their being, if they were to give up this sort of thing. First of all comes the desire to possess, then this clinging to what they have identified themselves with: out of this arises cupidity and then pride (2 Tim 3:2).

Such a person is necessarily unfree, for this thing that has in fact reached him from outside, with which he has identified himself – whether it is love or money, or success or fear, or fear of embarrassment or what you will – is of course always what might be taken away from him: he sees then that it is not in fact absolutely identical with himself and that it must therefore be defended. Hence arises this ultimate lack of freedom, this unrest, this rushing about, this mistrust, this ambitiousness, this blindness. We need not assume at all that the happiness or wealth, with which the avaricious, proud person identifies himself, must from the very first be something sinful; but in a case of conflict, he can cling to all this only in a sinful way. The result is impiety, because it is only as a free agent – that is, by never identifying himself absolutely with one particular good – that anyone can be free. Only in this way can the *Deus semper major* be known to man and remain in him.

From all this we could deduce other aspects of sin. If someone absolutely identifies himself with any kind of required good, he is of course – at least in the long run – in no position to admit that he is culpably clinging to something sinful. He will necessarily draw up new lists of values which provide him with a justification for acting in the way he has chosen and for remaining in the same state. He will create his own system of values, he will adapt standards so as to put himself in the right; he will suppress his guilt, mask his conscience: for if he identifies himself with this good that can be retained only by sin, he cannot at the same time admit that he is living in a false situation, maintaining a wrong decision. A real identity is established between the innermost reality of the person and the false standards of the good that is to be condemned and rejected. Then guilt begins at the point where the person claims to have a good conscience.

4. *The making of a true christian*

Ignatius then describes the making of a true christian (146): poverty as confidence in God alone, courage for God, leaving behind any other value. In the world this means first of all breakdown, ignominy. It means becoming somehow meaner, poorer, perhaps stupid, cheated, apparently backward and useless, apparently exploited, weak. Don't think of riches in this connection, since this only conceals the real issue for us today. Take perhaps the example of a conflict between subject and superior in a radical, serious matter. Anyone who gives up at this point his honour, his freedom, his love, must at first feel that he is falling into chaos and that it is pointless to take the risk. Nowhere in his experience will he have the impression of being rewarded for it. According to the sermon on the mount (Mt 5:3–12), he is one who mourns, who suffers persecution, and so on. But in this void left free in his heart through forsaking everything, believing without seeing, giving up things without being directly rewarded: in this existential and not merely theoretical transcendence the *Deus semper major* really comes to be known and only in this way.

There is really an immediate, primal relationship to God as the ground of our existence, which is not yet thematic or conceptual. This primal relationship exists *ratione naturae*: it is a transcendence to God that is always and necessarily being realised in virtue of existence; but it exists – that is, it should exist – *ratione personae*, in mentally free existence. There this transcendence to God is really established in a free decision and cannot be established except by leaving behind a finite good, which at first gives the impression that we must be identified with it and that without it we cannot live and be. When this is given up, when man in the power of grace has the courage to leave it behind, although he will get no reward; the courage to remain silent, although he will then seem stupid; to give way, although he gains nothing by it and his sacrifice is taken for granted; to renounce something, although it seems to break his heart and make life no longer worth living: whenever this transcendence and the transcendence of a created, earthly spirit really occurs in absolute freedom, in an absolute leap without security, then there comes to be that which Ignatius means when he speaks of poverty, humility, as the dawning upon us of the *Deus semper major*.

178

5. *Assimilation to Christ*

After considering these two attitudes, it should be made clear that they can be confused on the emotional and secular plane. Poverty can be misunderstood as supreme, cool indifference to possessions. A longing to be scorned and despised may be a way of seeking attention. Arrogance can appear in the clothing of humility, as the attitude of someone who can afford to be the impassive servant of all. Therefore this will to be poor, humiliated, humbled, as opposed to the desire – as a satanic temptation – for possessions, notice, being, needs again to be reduced to a will to the humility of ordinariness, of the duty that everyone does, in which no one sees anything special. What is required is adaptation to the ordinary routine of the church – for example, exercising humility in letting others be noticed – and finally getting away from oneself and everything else, by having the childlike courage to leave the last word and judgment to God.

Finally, this attitude, described here in a very formal and philsophical manner, ought to be seen as specifically christian, that is, as our share in that becoming poor, that abandonment of self, that being stripped of any apparent content, which Jesus Christ, the crucified, accomplished when in poverty, pain, ignominy, in the God-forsakenness of his death, in absolute obedience, not seeking notice, and poverty, not seeking possessions, he gave himself up into the hands of the incomprehensible God: the God who is not to be summed up in advance, who cannot be included in our calculations. What Ignatius wants to tell us in the meditation on the two standards is accomplished in these deeds of the crucified Christ.

17 THE THREE CLASSES OF MEN

For the second meditation on election we shall make use of the text of St Ignatius on the "three classes of men" (149–157).

1. *The function of the meditations on election*

It is a question of meditations on election since Ignatius sees the whole of the *Exercises* as an election, and therefore wants to guide man to the right disposition for making his actual choice. The general disposition was laid down in the *Foundation*, since it is established there already that there must be a will for the "more" in the sense of the objectively better means, a will therefore to indifference, to be dissociated from things in order to be able to appreciate them simply for what they are: in the words of the *Imitation of Christ, sapere res prouti sunt.*

It is true that, according to the *Foundation* of the *Exercises*, the will of God could clearly coincide with the objective, attainable state of affairs, might be precisely the better co-ordination of the end with a particular, perfectly apt means. Ignatius does not stop at this.

In the first week man was acknowledged to be a sinner: just because he is only a sinner, he is delivered up unconditionally to God's providence. He knows that, as a human being, he can count in no way on what God might do and that the God whom he faces is the greater, so that the partnership and covenantal relationship between God and man are not between equals. In a way, man always has to surpass himself in his quest for God. But God, in his absolute, uncontrollable transcendence, always remains the greater. Thus in the ultimate relationship of man to God this fulfilment of his will cannot unambiguously and completely be reduced to the question of what is the objectively better means in itself, and how this is to be chosen. This God appeared in the first week as merciful love in person, by whom man may and must permit himself to be loved: as the God of a supernatural life, of an absolute self-communication, in which God as the infinite, incalculable, uncontrollable, as the absolute mystery, comes into man's life. We are also faced – for instance, in the colloquy of mercy (61) – with God as the crucified Lord, seeking to win our love, since he himself shares our importance and need.

In the course of the first week, a "more" was already established which is not simply identical with the almost rational "more" of the objectively better means and thus with pure indifference, which are mentioned in the *Foundation*. In the meditation on Christ's kingdom man perceives the evangelical call: this meditation is not merely a pious reflection which we choose to make. The basic outline of the gospel, of the christian faith itself, is expressed here. In the meditation on Christ's kingdom, it is a question of a call – to which an offer on our side corresponds – to imitate Christ our Lord in his historical situation, so that the person of Christ becomes the law of our life, so that beyond all objective substantiation he is the crucified one, calling us to toil, suffering and death.

This election situation then is no longer simply man's

181

determination to choose according to his own standards what is objectively better and therefore to remain
indifferent in regard to such an objective choice. There
is really established a will to a personal love for that
greater, uncontrollable, incalculable God, who is not
simply identical with the objective structures of the
world, with the calculable diversities of the means. A
will to Jesus Christ, the crucified, is already involved
in this love.

Something still more sublime is meant by the three
classes of men. What counts now is the free, unreserved
surrender to God's supreme love, over and above any
special consideration of the matter in hand, even beyond all love of the cross. The better which is now in
question is the decision of divine love, itself free and
incalculable, one way or the other. This means – we
can't alter this at all, it is Ignatian theology, Ignatian
metaphysics and asceticism – that the decision which
we are seeking here is no longer attainable with the
aid of purely rational means or purely objective appropriate principles.

It is no longer a question of choosing the objectively better means, of simply taking on the heavier
cross of our Lord, in the clarity of greater suffering,
pain, and greater renunciation but, over and above all
this, everything is left once again to God, for him to
decide, for him to proclaim his will. Thus the wholly
individual decision results from God's freedom in
greatness and power, and then calls forth this free
movement of love for God, in which man is really
exposed on all sides to the pure providence of God. In
all this of course there is presupposed as possible, as
worth seeking and conceivable, a knowledge of God's

will of which our moral theology has remarkably little to say.

At the same time, this pure, absolute surrender to God's love and its dominion over us, which is no longer within our power to calculate, beyond all objective reflection and love of the cross, in this meditation on the three classes of men, is once again anchored in a realistic common-sense, in the routine situation where all this achievement must take place: the creator really deals directly with the creature, beyond all abstract norms – without of course denying or abolishing these – and proclaims to the creature his holy will, which is the imparting of his divine love.

2. *The men's situation*

Consider first the situation in which St Ignatius places these three men or groups of men. In our reflections we may assume that, instead of the ten thousand ducats, each person or group holds an office. They are supposed to have obtained this office legitimately. In the light of a strictly relevant, objectivist ethic, the office itself is perfectly justified in the sight of God. Those who hold the office are right to exercise it: it is an objectively proper service of God and human nature finds fulfilment in it. But the office has not been acquired out of love of God.

At this point we stop short: St Ignatius evidently assumes that things in our life which are humanly and morally legitimate may always be re-examined to see whether they have been acquired out of love for God. Although we are normally not particularly spiritually minded, we do in fact judge our life according to its conformity or otherwise to God's will in a given situation. As soon as it appears not to contradict God's will, we are inclined to think that we have a free rein and our conscience is clear. We might say that it is simply impossible in our life for everything, all our human reality, *in actu secundo*, effectively to spring originally from our love of God. This sounds abstruse. But in fact it is clear that we can only begin to love God after we have come to be, after we have had laid upon us a quite particular existence: our endowments, the circumstances of our life, people around us, the historical, social and cultural situation of our time.

With our freedom of decision, with our love of God which we want to realise, we find ourselves already in a situation which has not of itself arisen out of our love for God and which is not simply the realisation and objectification of this love: we are already everything possible. We already do a great deal, we have already reached out to all that is possible, we have perhaps taken up an attitude of reserve to a thousand things, internal and external, in our life, before the question can arise at all of whether this comes about through love of God. To this extent it is true that the task of taking everything so to speak into the depths of love and making a start from there outwards is one which can be achieved only slowly – if at all – over a whole life-time.

In other words, we are from the first full of unrelated possibilities, with impulses and attitudes which are far from being so integrated inwardly that everything springs out of this one love. This does not mean of course that so much has been given to us prior in time and nature to our love that this love could not also be the source of all these things. When, for example, someone absolutely accepts his modest talents, when he succeeds in integrating his natural capacity – which he cannot brush aside – into the pure act of love of God, in grace he permits this love to enter deeply into him, these things too – given in advance, unavoidable and impossible to shed – grow out of his love.

This absolute integration, however, of all elements of our mental existence into the love of God, so that everything springs from this love, is something that we have never yet completely accomplished. Figuratively speaking, we have never yet loved God "with all our heart, with all our soul" (Mt 22:37), we have not loved out of the whole reality of our existence, so that now all that is in us, all that we have and do, is the realisation and objectification of this love. Nevertheless this does not mean that love imposes a claim, binding in some sense under pain of sin. It means that love is a criterion, a measure, of our life, imposed in the gospel by Jesus Christ, who precisely in this way overcomes the dogmas, the ethic based on agreements, the ethic of achievement, of the old testament.

For the most part however we do not feel that we have a duty to integrate our whole life into the love of God – and this disturbs us. This is what Ignatius presupposes with these three men or groups of men, with their money or their office. They have reached a stage at which they are really disturbed in regard to a particular reality in their life, in so far as this is not integrated into the love of God and does not exist as an element in this all-embracing love shaping and penetrating everything. They feel that there is something in their life which is not the realisation of what is absolutely first and last: from man's standpoint, his

freedom; from God's, his spirit. They feel therefore a
still unformed alien element within their christian life
as spirit-persons and thus in a wholly mysterious
fashion this thing which in itself is quite legitimate, this
honest calling, this money completely honestly acquired, appears as pressure on and hindrance to this
pure realisation of love.

3. The men's reflections

These men then ask themselves what they must do.
What are these three to do? Ignatius says that all three
want to save their souls. They do not think of this salvation of the soul as opposed to the will of God. They
want salvation to come about in virtue of the legitimate will of the creature in regard to itself, but as in
accordance with the will of God. In itself the salvation of souls is not made impossible and not placed in
jeopardy by these disturbing pressures.

We must turn back to the meditation on the two
standards. This thing which is possible in itself, not *a
priori* contrary to God's will, is however of itself something ambivalent and can therefore become one of the
impediments described in the meditation on the two
standards. This legitimate decision, not in itself contrary to the soul's salvation, can in fact be felt as an
impediment and a danger, at least as a task not yet
finished and mastered, since it is not absolutely integrated into the original effort of will to God, incorporating everything into itself. Hence these three men
rightly continue to fear for their soul's salvation.

Ignatius says that these men want simply to find God
and in fact to find him in everything. They recognise
therefore that what is morally legitimate and possibly

salutary is a real task for them, a task still facing them. They want then to find God himself also in their office. It is just this reality which should become transparent, should become a positive factor in their loving, absolute self-realisation to God. This is only another way of saying that this reality is being integrated in some way into their life as a positive factor. The integration is not yet achieved, but it is already being sought. All then reach out for this supreme ideal, for all the reality of their lives to be inwardly, positively filled with God, transparent to God, and for all their resources therefore not to be wasted in different directions, but to be concentrated in this one direction on God, in order to find God in everything. In other words, everything else is to be found only in God and in his love.

It is of course clear that this is the task of a whole lifetime and that it is never finished as long as we remain pilgrims on this earth. We are not talking about reaching a certain level of asceticism, but of a task which requires a whole lifetime by the very fact that man is constantly faced with new realities. This is how it will always be with us; this is why we begin to think too that we are becoming more and more imperfect. Why? Because new things continue to come before us in an increasingly urgent way, constantly presenting new and more radical questions, presenting us with unfinished tasks, tasks still to be accomplished.

The greater the range of what man genuinely sees as what could express his love for God, and the less things in his life appear to be clear and obvious (as they are likely to appear to young and immature people, even when christian) or as something about which nothing can be done (like the shape of his nose), so much the more will the christian feel himself overwhelmed by the task that faces him: that immensity and incalculability of the love of God which is in fact the peculiar feature of the religion in which God himself has become the inner principle and so too the ultimate standard and challenge for man.

It is in this frame of mind and with this will that these three men are faced with this task. They want to get rid of the pressure, the obstacle, the rawness, the opacity, of these things – internal and external – in their life, so that love may take hold on a greater part of that life and subdue it.

In this situation two things appear to be really possible. In this respect we must note that Ignatius presents the case as a question of money, of an office, of a livelihood, something it is physically possible to eliminate from a person's life. This of course is not the only possible case: there are ultimate problems of existence that simply cannot be eliminated. A person observes that he is incurably ill or that he is faced quite simply with a task which, with the best will in the world, he is incapable of mastering in the way he would like to; someone is involved from the beginning in a conflict of obedience with his superiors, who require from him something that he finds very difficult. Situations like this, which cannot be solved merely by giving up something, have to be considered in this meditation. How precisely they link up with Ignatius' basic scheme is something about which we need not bother our heads further here. At any rate, Ignatius thinks that the problem can be solved by the person's detaching himself from the thing in a heroic leap or fusing it into his decision for God.

In principle two solutions are possible: assimilation, integration of the matter in hand into the love of God, thus achieving mastery of the problem, or complete detachment from the matter. The first solution makes sense, the second is heroic. But the selection between these two is not within man's power. The choice between the two relevant solutions, objectively possible in the light of an essential morality, according to Ignatius, is reserved to God and his decision, and man must submit to this free will of God which comes upon him and is by him incalculable.

Ignatius does not decide the choice for his retreatants in this meditation, but prepares them for it. It is a question first of all directly of neither the one nor the other, but of the free, loving surrender to the love of God in the pure will of God and of the pure "dispose of me" (234). When this will of God is accomplished, it can be accomplished in either way. This of course does not mean that the objective decision in actual cases becomes irrelevant. It may well be that, prior to a question put in this way, the situation is already of such a character that the question is decided in the light of the matter in hand and of a particular situation of choice. If someone is faced with the question whether to become a teacher or not and knows that he is incompetent or that he could present a moral danger to children, the problem is already decided objectively in the light of the objective rightfulness or wrongfulness of the means or situation in question. But we are talking here of a situation of a more sublime kind, where the decision properly so called can never wholly and adequately be settled in the light of the objective circumstances, but is either simply the person's autonomous choice or the result of his placing himself in a perfect way at the disposal of this absolute, personal will of God which is beyond any objective calculation. These three in fact are aware of all this. Ignatius now describes what they do.

4. *The men's decision*

The first wants pure love, love that integrates everything; out of his life with all its elements he wants to make a pure hymn of praise to the divine majesty and he wants to integrate into this achievement of his life everything that is in him and is to remain in him. But this man is lethargic, he does nothing, Ignatius says. He will not bring himself to take the risk of unconditional love. It is not a question yet of lacking the courage to cut himself off from this particular thing, but what he lacks from the very start is the courage simply to love and to place himself unconditionally at the disposal of the Other. Why? Because he fears the immensity of this love of God, which can be life or death, or any other thing; because he does not love the greater unconditionally, will not surrender himself; because he clings to salvation.

This does not mean that man should or could renounce his salvation, but here it is pinned down in such a way that the God who is always greater than all is not himself allowed to rule unreservedly, absolutely, in utter simplicity. The result is that nothing happens, no means is chosen nor is any decision really made; for this inertness before this possibility essentially means that no real election of a positive character takes place in regard to the good in question. Everything remains vague, unsettled up to the moment of death.

What happens then, we are not told here.

The second man wants to love God, he wants to be loved infinitely by God; in a true and genuine sense, aware of this basic problem of his life, he wants to integrate into the love of God all that belongs to his life; but he wants God's love for him and his love for God – both – to be realised as the effect of his own unrestricted, autonomous decision. He does not want to go to God unconditionally, but to decide for himself the way in which he will find God in all things. Office every time will be for him decisive: one way or the other. He wants to dictate to God to give him the opportunity, the strength, the inner spontaneity, to integrate all his reality into the love of God, but only in such a way that what he has willed is still retained. This person, then, will not admit that the apparently pointless abandonment of something which can be appropriately co-ordinated is also a genuine opportunity of loving God, a phenomenon of groundless love of the cross, full of the folly and emptiness of God.

This man's attitude is that of the second degree of humility. He will give up a particular earthly good only when it is proved that it cannot work otherwise. Forsaking something is what he sees, as if in a sense bewitched, and he does not look to God and his love, before whom "forsaking" and "retaining" can be existentially indifferent, and do then become so for this man, so that he can really leave them at God's disposal, leave to him the last word: a word that is beyond his calculations, based solely on the importance or unimportance of the matter.

The third man has that love which freely leaves everything to God, without any preference, prepared for both alternatives. Nor has he any preference for forsaking possessions, for asceticism, for renunciation. It is of course only through the grace of Christ's cross that a man, still in the grip of sin and concupiscence, can attain such an attitude. In so far as he has managed this, he comes in the long run through the self-denying sacrificial love of the cross to that attitude of absolutely free detachment, in which are included once again the renunciation, the cross, the death of the God who still remains the greater even in the fate of his Son.

This third person in fact is faced with the free groundlessness of love of the God who is always greater, of love which really has no other criterion than that of its own inscrutable freedom. A love that can reveal itself in what way it will and thus gives man the opportunity to make his own love real by forsaking or retaining, integrating or excluding, a particular reality. For this third person therefore, still a pilgrim, this attitude of love freely given is something still to be attained, to be struggled for, to be prayed for, and he has to endure the struggle to make himself free from this inner attachment to the thing – and this is always difficult. In order to get free (157) he must pray for the actual requirement and obligation to give it up. But it is in this light alone that calculation, readiness, looking for a way of giving up the thing – all of which left the two former men lethargic – become truly possible.

The third type of person is no longer shocked at the idea of giving up things, for he is really caught up by the sovereign love of God raising him above them all. This love alone stirs him. It is God who deals directly with his creature. Here it can truly be said, "the kingdom of God is at hand" (Mk 1:15), in retaining or forsaking, in life and in death. Here man has really become the loving child, looking directly to God and permitting the sovereign, unfathomable freedom of God to be decisive, just because he is loved. Therefore he no longer finds anything shocking even in the plurality of things, into which this incomprehensible infinity of God is placed within the world in creatureliness and createdness.

5. *Colloquies*

In the light of this we can understand the triple colloquy (156). The first to Mary who said: "Let it be to me according to your word" (Lk 1:38). That and nothing else. Everything else is related to this, is recognised as the manifestation in plurality of one and the same love of God and is seen as an equally possible realisation of the one love, so that we really can accept from God just whatever he chooses to give.

It is obvious that Jesus, his cross and his death, his life too, which is life altogether in the fullness of all God-created reality, is model, enablement, and norm. Hence the prayer to this Jesus.

Finally, the colloquy with the Father, whose love is beyond all rational explanation and in its freedom and proper nature is the reason for everything else, has no other standard above or alongside it by which it might be calculated. This alone is the love which embraces all things. Only when by God's grace we confront this love with an unreserved "Yes" and so become free from ourselves and all that otherwise constitutes us, are we the men, the christians, the priests, that we ought to be.

18 THE THREE KINDS OF HUMILITY

Ignatius suggests that it is useful to consider the three kinds of humility (165–168); we can very well make a meditation on this.

1. *Humility and love*

Ignatius calls these three ways of behaving in regard to God and to Jesus Christ our Lord three degrees or kinds of humility. He might well have described them also as three kinds of love: for it is really the same thing. When Ignatius speaks of election, he really means the election-attitude, the enduring basis of decision, and this in fact is the purest love for God, the ever-greater, and for Jesus Christ, the crucified. Indifference as openness for the greater service of God, for the better, for the absolutely free ordinance of divine love, is in fact itself love. Ignatius calls this attitude humility evidently because it is the love which is due precisely to God as the greater, the incomprehensible, the one who rules our lives; it is the clear attitude of the creature in face of the incomprehensible God, in which love in fact once again takes on a quite special shape: not love as an obvious self-offering, not a love drawing its possibility and power from our own resources.

2. *Basic decision*

In his description of the three kinds of humility, Ignatius presupposes the distinction between venial and mortal sin. We know from theology that there is an objective distinction and that there can also be a subjective distinction. In the actual situation of an actual human being, who can never adequately reflect on himself, in the light also of theology and of human experience, it must be admitted that this objectively existing and subjectively realisable distinction between venial and mortal sin is not as simple as it first seems.

We may recall the fact that there are fundamental decisions in human life which perhaps cannot be made objectively explicit at all; we may recall that human life cannot be broken down into individual acts, but really has an inner existential unity. In the light of this we can see that a total basic decision in the depth of human nature may be wrong and indeed gravely sinful without there necessarily being a grave total lapse in the sight of God. We may recall that such a basic decision does not *ipso facto* turn every later act into a grave sin in the strict sense, but nevertheless integrates the rest of a person's acts into its wrongfulness, uses the good also once again as a means to evil, even though the seizure of this particular good as such need not be a grave sin on that account. From all this it is clear that we must be rather careful about applying these objectively correct concepts – that is, the distinction between mortal and venial sin – in our personal ascetic life.

3. *The three degrees*

With regard to the three degrees or kinds of humility, we must observe first of all that they are all given positive value by Ignatius. The description of the degrees here does not mean that the lower degrees are inferior or bad, just because they can and should be overcome on the way to the higher: quite the contrary. All three degrees are to be given positive value, are open to one another; in their threefold unity they form the one entire basic attitude of the person and are constantly mutually dependent on each other. They are three vital movements of one and the same person in regard to God, continually merging into one another, and only in this merging into one another, in their mutual openness and independence, constitute the one, entire, holy, healthy attitude of man to God.

a) *The first degree*

The first degree is described by Ignatius as love that starts out unpretentiously from below. It is an absolute determination to accept God's will, so far as God wills himself as man's end and destines man for himself as the one, real and true end (this is what the question of grave sin and its avoidance means).

Already in the first degree, the human will enters absolutely and unambiguously into the rhythm of this absolute will of God for himself as the unique personal, infinite, supernatural end. This already is something great and glorious of which we must always ask whether in fact it does exist in the depth of our nature. Can we say that we are justified, sanctified by God, anointed and sealed by his Spirit, that we are believers – people whose ultimate, mental horizon shaping everything else is the eternal truth of God himself – that we are those who know by faith together with God's Spirit. If this is so, then we can say that we are those who hope, those whose dynamism – in spite of all the diversity of our endeavours, in spite of the fact that not all the resources of our nature are yet integrated into the love of God – is still in the last resort oriented to God; we can say that the Holy Spirit of love is poured into our hearts (Rom 5:5).

If only we are granted this grace, we are already the greatly loved children of God; we are not only called this, we are such(1 Jn 3:1). We are those who in the ultimate depths of their nature possess the reality of God in an absolute self-communication, who live from God and for him. Then, although everything else in us is human, earthly, ordinary, mean, monotonous, this would be and is the last thing that is to be said of us.

This unpretentious love of God, starting out so to speak from the matter in hand, from the commandments of God, from the world, in the form of an absolute determination for God as last end, is in practice however a love that accepts what comes as a manifestation of God's will; it is not an exuberant love racing towards God. It is love for God, wholly sustained by the Holy Spirit of God, which nevertheless learns from the concrete situation what is necessary to attain this goal and to maintain our orientation to the goal. This is an unassuming love: it waits, it does not hurl itself into adventures, it acquires the concept of its realisation from the internal and external circumstances as they happen to be.

Hence it is clear that these three forms of humility are not simply piled on top of each other: for up to a point this unassuming love arising out of the world, starting out from below, is something essential to man. Over large stretches of life he cannot act otherwise. He must wait. He must learn from the circumstances of his life what is to be done here and now. With the best will in the world, he cannot expect merely from his own resources to bring about here and now this final, most sublime integration of the whole human reality into the love of God. We do not have such power over ourselves.

The greatness of this first degree of humility lies in the fact that the justified person, the child of God, the heir of eternal life and the brother of Jesus Christ is already present. The hard fact however – and therefore also necessary – is that to a large extent such an attitude is simply unavoidable for the temporal, historical creature unable to dispose of his own life. The dangerous feature of this situation lies in the fact that this still spontaneous, naturally positive attitude towards creatures, not yet finally purified by indifference, can always reach a point at which sin appears unambiguously as grave.

b) *The second degree*
The second degree is that of the love which liberates us from ourselves, the degree of active indifference. Someone who possesses the first kind of love finds himself in harmony with the world and with worldly things, inside and outside man, is also unaware of any problem here, waits – so to speak – to see if a situation requiring a decision will arise, and therefore hopes that all will go well because he will still have time to dissociate himself from things. A person who possesses the second degree of humility has already recognised that it is really worthier of God and himself to create an active zone of indifference in which he is able to dissociate himself from apparently obvious things in the world, in order so much the more clearly,

decisively, distinctly to be able to make his choice for God. It is obvious that the second person is translating all this directly into moral terms and that he has the will to avoid every so-called venial sin. For, to the extent that he possesses this active indifference, he dissociates himself from those intramundane realities, from those means to the end, in which the Thomistic tradition saw the possible occurrence of what is known as venial sin; for venial sins, according to this teaching, are offences not in regard to the ends, but in regard to the means.

Anyone who possesses this active indifference of a love that liberates him, so that he is able to love God impartially through the world, is to that extent protected against venial sin. At the same time, it must always be pointed out that this absolute, active indifference as real and not merely accepting what has to be is something that we never possess perfectly, but towards which – at best – we are moving. Hence the greatness and significance of this second form of love becomes obvious. It is free, active indifference, which produces a free gaze towards God as such. God becomes known in a radical way, existentially, transcendentally, and not merely categorically. This love is achieved here in a synthesis, always already established, of God and his will with particular things in the world.

Of course there is a constant return from this second kind of love into the first. Man always becomes aware of himself as already existing in the world and after a choice has been made. Indifference in the sense of complete neutrality and undecidedness simply does not exist for the finite creature. In theory it existed or might have existed at the moment before we made a choice for the first time with absolute personal freedom. But when was that? How? It is beyond recall.

This first beginning of our freedom is forever outside the scope of our reflection. We cannot say when it was that we decided for the first time for or against God; it is impossible to recall when we began for the first time freely to love something and so to get rid of this indifference, even though there was no question of sin. Looking back then it is clear that this supremely free indifference has already been pierced and merged in the first degree of humility—or of love. Moreover, in human life new situations are always arising, new goods are always confronting us, new experiences of freedom always lie before us, as a result of a planning and a direction that is not our own: all these things undoubtedly exercise an attraction and have inevitably already absorbed something of our active indifference before we can really apply our freedom. You learn this in the course of your ordinary life. It is only at a comparatively late stage that we first notice how much we depend on something, how completely we are already identified with it.

This second degree of humility therefore is not to be found in absolute purity; it simply cannot be. There is then necessarily a return from this will of active indifference to the humility of the first degree of love, in which a man allows the world, fate, the great ones appointed by God, to rule over him and trusts that even the unplanned, unforeseen, that which is not calculated in the light of an attitude of sovereign freedom, will still turn out to his good (Rom 8:28).

If you want this spelled out, it might be said: if we

could have an adequate, hundred per cent active indifference, then there could not be any merely sufficient
graces; but then the Molinist God in his freedom would
have to observe almost with regret and amazement that
he could place us in any conceivable situation and yet
our heroic, absolute indifference to any conceivable
good which might take us by surprise would mean that
we had no difficulty in making the right choice. From
this standpoint also we see how this active indifference
of a love fighting to gain an area of freedom simply
cannot be the complete destiny of a created, poor,
temporal human being implanted in the world from
the very beginning, and thus in fact there is a constant
return from the second to the first degree of humility. It
must then always be admitted that to a certain extent
the incalculable, unforceable grace of God has to save
us in the first degree of humble love.

c) *The third degree*

The third degree is bold love for the cross of Christ
which, of itself, whenever it can, whenever it is not forbidden, positively reaches out for poverty, shame,
humiliation, the cross of Christ. Ignatius means here
to describe an attitude in which the danger of a failure
to understand the true will of God is to be overcome.
Undoubtedly, this bold love of the cross, of shame, of
poverty, of Christ's death, is the best defence against
a failure to understand the true will of God as a result
of an unadmitted self-love.

We might well reflect on our own position in regard
to this love of the cross, this love of the "folly of the
cross" (1 Cor 1:23). First of all it can be said that it is
not easy for us to appreciate the significance for ourselves

of the lot of Jesus as we can understand it from his life. Merely because we want to love Jesus with our whole heart, merely because this love is a really personal one, it does not follow that it will be easy to be convinced that therefore shame too, poverty, humiliation, must not only be patiently accepted when God's command imposes them on us, but must themselves be sought.

The depth-psychologists also know something of this: there can also be a false craving for humiliation which shows itself in the oddest ways. Let us ask ourselves whether it is so obvious without more ado that to love Jesus is the same as wanting nothing other than him. Do we rouse that personal, direct love—rising above all abstractions of fundamental relationships with Christ—which makes this concrete life—not the hypostatic union and other ultimate causes of our salvation, but the established fact of this life—the norm? Can we say that, if we love him, that to which we feel drawn consists in this voluntary election—whenever God gives me the opportunity and the right—of what is difficult, humiliating, of abasement, poverty, hardship?

Even if these questions are not easy to answer, we must observe unemotionally and objectively that the incarnation establishes a relationship in which Jesus Christ is a norm of our life which properly speaking cannot be judged by a higher norm. I cannot say—for instance—in the light of this higher norm that there is a point at which I could perhaps share Jesus' suffering, but which certainly from the first is out of the question for me. Setting aside all ascetic and trite formularies, consider the case of a woman who loves her husband with her whole heart and knows that he has cancer, that he is incurable, lost: she would want to have cancer herself, she would not want an easier lot than her husband. Perhaps people in former times felt this involuntarily. Can we claim that this logic of love is so obvious to us? Nevertheless we have to say quite unemotionally in theological terms that Jesus Christ with his actual life is the law of our life.

This however does not mean that every detail of his life is to be copied literally and directly in our life. Nevertheless, the problem then arises as to how – for example – the poverty, humiliation, persecution, and the rest of Jesus' sufferings are to be imitated by us, if we cannot in fact copy the actual details. There is a limit here which cannot be clearly marked in a rational and reflex way. We shall have to be content with the two purely theoretical statements: first, the concrete life of Jesus is the final norm of our life, not to be judged by any higher norm; second, we cannot and may not simply copy Jesus, because it is precisely in our own situation that we must continue the life of Jesus in a new way, because we must represent in new historical situations in our christian life the fullness of his Spirit which could not be given adequate objective expression even in Jesus' historicity, so that Jesus really does continue to live to the end of time in those who belong to him.

In our present situation, in our flight from suffering, our fear of the cross, our too slight love for Jesus, the crucified, we must reflect on how we are to achieve this third degree of humility. We have already seen that these three degrees must always be merging into one another. We know now that this readiness to go ahead, actively to seize on renunciation, sacrifice, death, cannot be the sole norm: that would be buddhism. We know that a positive relationship to earthly values and goods is not merely permitted to christians, but is an essential part of the christian life; that it can be a question therefore in the christian life merely of a dosage of that dialectical element which belongs essentially to christianity: to love the world and yet to despise it, to be able to esteem the world as the manifestation of God's glory and yet to be able to rise above it in a kind of indifference, in a love for the cross. These two attitudes are not merely permitted, but positively necessary for a christian life and therefore also for a priestly life.

4. Realisation of love of the cross

We have already seen that all this active love of the cross, all active attempts at renunciation, can in fact be nothing more than the exercise of that faith which is demanded in absolute sacrifice of every christian. Faith always means sacrificing the world in the confidence that the greater God of eternal life will make himself known to us and give us eternal life in this abandonment. This act as total surrender is required of every christian, at least in death. There the renunciation of the normal christian in the world and the renunciation of the religious reach one and the same summit, at which they have overcome themselves and all other things. We can never sacrifice more, forsake more, more actively dissociate ourselves from things than we do in death, when this is required of everybody.

This means however that love of the cross, without ascetic touching up, without ascetic jargon, once expressed and lived, is something that is imposed to an absolute degree in some way on every human being. Every man grows old, every man dies, every human life runs out at some point, every human life reaches its impassable frontier where man is no longer in possession of himself; every man experiences also infinite loneliness, the withdrawal of human love, the disappearance of all possible contacts however eagerly sought. What we call poverty, disgrace, humiliation, is nothing but a particular form of that which is imposed on every man in the depth of his existence. It can be given expression in these ascetic-positive terms only under two conditions: firstly, that these things are really accepted in our life at the point where they are imposed; secondly, that what we thus voluntarily accept and take to ourselves, what asceticism we decide on for ourselves, is understood as practice for that love of the cross which is finally required, which is asked of us, required of us, certainly in life's unavoidable death-trend, whether at that point we accept it or not.

It follows that this love of the cross in the third degree of humility is not something easy, that it obviously demands the greatest heroism on the part of the christian ascetic, but is nevertheless something that rises out of the inner structure of our existence. The saints in their lives constantly found and spoke of the fact that the penance they imposed on themselves was replaced in the course of time by a penance they had not sought, which they could not even have chosen voluntarily, which was much harder than anything else they had voluntarily undertaken in their lives.

It does not follow however that we can leave aside this autonomous love of the cross and renunciation, that what really matters will occur anyway and we need not trouble about this. For man is asked whether he trusts himself to maintain this real love of the cross where the cross is imposed and not sought, whether he there brings the radical heroism of faith, hope and love to bear, whether he now really accepts and understands this interpretation of life for this situation – which is primarily the cross of Christ – and makes it his life's structure. Since man must question himself in this way, since he must really have a salutary fear as to whether he will in fact manage this, he seizes voluntarily on the cross for testing and practice.

If I remain silent for once at some point, without excusing or defending myself, and permit an unjust judgment to rest on me, this is nothing special or very great. It would be a very odd interpretation of the christian life to suppose that this in itself and for its own sake constitutes the imitation of the crucified Christ. This holds even for someone who has voluntarily undertaken many penances and night vigils and heaven knows what. If someone does this as a christian, he does it all because of the urgent question: shall I really recognise and accept the cross of Christ as that which has been decided for me? Christ's own asceticism led to the very reproach that he did not do penance as the Baptist had done.

Jesus however approached the cross, the unsought, terrible, all-annihilating cross, forcing him into God-forsakenness. Because he took this path, because he did so quite spontaneously, in an absolutely active, clear way, he succeeded in practising actively (and this is the point of our love of the cross) what we must endure anyway in our life: for our life – humanly speaking – can break down, can end in disaster. We can and indeed we shall anyway die and, presumably, before death we shall have to suffer a long, sad decline of our powers;

however arrogantly we live, however rich we are humanly speaking, we shall feel at every point the finitenesses of our own life, of our own powers, we shall have to put up with the stupidity of people around us, we shall see the whole finiteness of the world, we shall experience the most bitter disappointments in our apostolate.

We are approaching all this inevitably. Over our whole life there lies what we call in ascetic jargon the cross of Christ. Love of the cross, the third degree of humility, is really imposed on us and in this sense has nothing at all to do with the enthusiasm of a superficial, emotional wishing to become like the crucified saviour. The cross in his life is much more than a painful façade. This same cross as the innermost existential in our life – this is how the third degree is rightly understood – sets two questions before us: Are you prepared to accept the place which God has assigned to the cross in your life as a participation in the lot of the incarnate, crucified God? Do you understand and have you the courage to recognise the necessity of practising and preparing for this final act of life, the hardest decision, the act of the most radical faith and of hope against all hope and of love of God which is manifested in your passing? Have you the courage to do this by constantly actively practising in your life the acceptance of the cross of Christ (not as the sole norm, not in immoderate asceticism)? If, out of such wholly personal love for the crucified Christ, a person manages to bring a greater inner ardour to this will to approach the necessary cross, so much the better.

19 EUCHARIST

In this context also it is a good thing to have a meditation on the eucharist: for it is a fact that we derive
little profit out of the daily celebration of the merciful
mystery of our faith. This may be said to be due simply
to the fact that we are at heart poor, lazy, weary, closed
up in ourselves. This is true up to a point, but it does
not explain how even the celebration of this mystery of
faith is more or less a routine affair, something we carry
out willingly and with faith, but which is covered by
the dust of the daily grind.

1. *Eucharist and ordinary life*

First of all, we may raise the question: Is it true that
in the eucharist, in offering the sacrifice and receiving
holy communion, that which is most wonderful and
unsurpassable in our life takes place? Or is the matter
a little less simple, when we look at it more precisely,
more truly, more calmly, in theological terms? The
answer to this question really has to be more complex.

The cross of Golgotha always overshadows and
hovers over our life. We are always living within sight
of this tree of life. God always looks out on us in his
merciful love from the cross. We are always sustained
by this event. The sacrifice of the mass is not what
brings us first of all into contact with the sacrifice of
the cross; but that which always holds for us and for
our life becomes visible in a substantial way, although
only sacramentally, in the sacrifice of the mass. Our

life is sustained by this act of obedience and love on
the part of the Son of God, so that this sacramental
anamnesis of the cross of Christ occurs as sacrifice in
the mass; but this does not mean that we enter into
a relationship with the cross of Christ only at these
moments of time in our life. Everywhere this cross sustains us; whenever man in belief, hope and love, reaches
out for God, he realises also this existential of his life,
the cross of Christ.

We receive in communion the true body of Christ
and drink his true blood, but this reception of the body
and blood is in fact the sacrament for a unification by
grace with Christ in his Spirit and the sacrament of an
increase by grace of this unity in Christ. This spiritual
unity in Christ and its increase and deepening (*res
sacramenti*) is the lasting, permanent gift of God to justified man. This increase, this existential acceptance of
unity with Christ in his life-giving Spirit, can in fact
occur in a more radical sense and in a way more important for salvation apart from the reception of the
sacrament which is the body of Christ. The reception
of the body of Christ is not only the fruit of the eucharist,
it is in particular also the effective sign of what occurs
and ought to occur as gift and task in the totality of
human life. Consequently the event of the mass and of
reception of communion must be seen from the first
within the totality of the christian life. No human being
can decide the moment when in our life there occurs
through grace, and supernaturally, the event in which
Christ is received adequately, absolutely, and as our
final salvation. The sacrament is not necessarily in this
sense the ultimately decisive factor of this salvation-
creating event.

The sacrament always helps towards this event, points to it, offers the necessary graces for it. But the cultic factor of the mass need not coincide with this most real and final event of our being and becoming christians, the definitive stage of our christian existence. From this standpoint, the sublimity of our supernaturally engraced life, in which the Holy Spirit intercedes for us with unutterable sighs (Rom 8:26), in which we are anointed and sealed by God himself (2 Cor 1:21–22), in which he lives his trinitarian life in the depths of our own nature, is concealed under the everyday labours, the greyness, the monotony of our human life. We need not be surprised therefore that the eucharist is also part of this situation of something believed and not – so to speak – comprehended, something for which we hope and not something already possessed for use in our whole christian life. We receive the bread of pilgrims and – to speak in old testament terms – receive it standing (Ex 12:11), as we enter into the daily routine; we receive it as weary, poor, oppressed pilgrims, believing that we are thus nourished for this life.

2. *Eucharist and divine worship*

Let us consider now the connection of the eucharist with divine worship and thus the connection of the eucharist as sacrifice with the ultimate task of creaturely existence: to adore God, to surrender oneself to him, to atone for sin. All this comes about through the sacrifice of the God-man on the cross. There, as the God-man, in the dignity of his divine-human person, he offered himself to the eternal Father, committed himself in a total surrender, in which this man Jesus Christ really succeeded in offering absolute indifference, absolute love, concentrating all the forces of his nature, in the acceptance of the absolute, incomprehensible decree of God the Father. What is constantly presented to me in the *Exercises* as the ideal of the nature of supernaturally engraced human beings, attainable only asymptotically, really came to be here.

This one total sacrifice of complete obedience, of absolute loyalty, as the concentration of all human resources supernaturally elevated in a single act, and this simultaneous plunging into the void of God-forsakenness, as a falling into the hands of the Father, took place on the cross and is present in the anamnesis of the mass: it is the sacrifice of the church, lovingly joining in the sacrifice of Christ, assembled to praise and adore the eternal majesty of the incomprehensible God. All this takes place under cultic, sacramental signs. It takes place whenever we hear and celebrate mass without sacrilege and of course with the necessary minimum of existential participation. But this very personal entry into the sacrifice of Christ on the cross has its peak in our actual wretched life and rarely indeed at the point where we put on our priestly vestments and celebrate the holy eucharist. It is in our ordinary dress, at our death-bed, in humiliation, in the steady fulfilment of our duty that this self-surrender occurs concretely and radically; there too the sacrifice takes place which we celebrate in fact with good will, but first of all liturgically, sacramentally in the mass. Hence our whole life is ultimately part of this eucharist as worship of God.

3. *Eucharist and growth in grace*

The eucharist is the sacrament of growth in grace, if we receive it sincerely – as well as we can – in faith, hope and love. But this growth in the eucharist as sacrament is only the initial sparking off of that growth in grace which comes about in life, in the real situations of faith, in hoping against all hope, and in the self-abandoning, self-overthrowing love which submits to the inscrutability of God's decree.

4. *Eucharist as sacrament of the church*

The eucharist is the sacrament of the church, not only in the sense that the church celebrates it, that every mass is an act of worship on the part of the holy community, but also in the sense that the church in this sacrament realises herself, accomplishes the sacramental expression and the effective sign of her unity and holiness and makes it present in her midst, so far as this is the sacrament of fraternal love and of the apostolate. This sacrifice attests, presupposes, requires, signifies and effects the unity of love in the church.

The local church is not merely an administrative area, a province of the church, but in a profound theological sense – as is obvious from Paul's terminology – it is itself the church, ultimately and seriously, because in this local congregation too, in this community of persons, the final and most profound self-realisation of the whole church occurs, namely, the eucharist. So this sacrifice is also naturally the source of love (1 Cor 11:29) and judgment on the presence or absence of our love of neighbour and on our priestly apostolate, because this charismatic, not merely administrative or institutional, priesthood of the new testament church must be sustained by this love of neighbour. If it is true that the eucharist is related in a radical sense directly and essentially to the unity of the church (1 Cor 10:17), to men's love of one another, if it is true that we are one body because we all share in the one bread, then the celebration of mass is necessarily the source of or the judgment on the actual form of our love of neighbour, which is the very thing in which our priestly mission consists.

5. *Proclamation of the death of Christ*

The eucharist as sacrament is also the proclamation of the death of Christ: "You proclaim the Lord's death until he comes" (1 Cor 11:26). We receive the body which was given for us, the blood that was shed for us. This silent sacrament, this Lord who permits himself to be sacramentally consumed, this sacrament proclaiming the death of Christ is also the "Yes" to the cross of Christ in our life, the sacrament of what we know as the third degree of humility. "We are always being given up to death for Jesus' sake" (2 Cor 4:11), as he was "offered because it was his own will" (Is 53:7 Vulgate). Those who constantly celebrate this eucharist "go forth to him outside the camp, bearing abuse for him" (Heb 13:13); the words *recolitur memoria passionis ejus* are really true. Here is the sacramental and official but also existentially necessary *anamnesis* of the passion of Christ. We are not only immersed in his death, we not only grow together with him through the likeness in his death (Rom 6:3–5), but our mass remains the sacrament of our readiness and power for suffering all that we have to accept calmly and objectively as the sacrifice which belongs to our calling.

6. *Sacrament of humanity*

This sacrament is also the sacrament of humanity. We receive the body of the Lord. We might also recall Tertullian's words: *Caro cardo salutis*. The body, transfigured matter, the risen body, is still something that belongs to this earth, since unity with the material creation from its roots upwards is so essential that it can never be completely broken. Not even God can so tear away a piece from this material world as to leave it without any internal connection with its former environment.

This corporality is the sign of our humanness: for "flesh" in the biblical sense means material, earthly, suffering, dying human beings; the whole man, in fact, the corporeal person at the mercy of earthly powers. If then Jesus speaks of the "body" (Mt 26:26) which he gives us, he means himself as a whole, in this concrete sense. But in this way our corporality itself becomes the sacrament of divine grace. This means too that divine grace exercises and can exercise its influence perfectly only by saving, transfiguring, finalising and confirming also the natural humanity of our human existence. To this extent, we can safely say, the sacrament is in this narrower sense a sacrament of humanity: for it gives the grace of Christ which, by healing, transfiguring, affirming, finalising our human existence, saves, sanctifies and confirms it, with all that belongs to it.

7. *Sacrament of holiness*

This sacrament is also the sacrament of holiness,

"medicine of immortality" (Ignatius of Antioch), pledge of future glory, sign foretelling eternal glory, anticipation under the sacramental sign of what one day will be final: the eucharist of eternal life.

8. *Starting point and centre of priestly life*

The sacrifice of the mass in a Benedictine, liturgical sense cannot always be at the centre of our life as much as we might think, nor is this possible or necessary from the nature of the catholic priesthood. But since the *res sacramenti* is celebrated in our whole life and that which really constitutes our life appears in the sacrament and in the sacrifice of the mass in a cultic form, and since this sacramental phenomenon is entrusted to the ministerial priest in the church, we can say in a completely true theological sense that the mass is the centre of our priestly existence. This is so even though in regard to our own life the mass has its centre at the point where man surrenders himself to God absolutely with the whole force of his concentrated love, where the christian has really grasped and seized on the cross of Christ. Nevertheless, we can say that the eucharist is the sacrament of our priestly life. The question facing us is this: Is our life such that this celebration is really a truthful sign also for us? Do we celebrate this sign in such a way that what we do liturgically in the mass really shows itself in our life?

Paul says that the liturgy of christians is the worship of our whole life and there we are poured out as a kind libation (Phil 2:17). This is truly an expression that applies or ought to apply to us, to our priestly life, and thus to what we do at mass.

20 THE PASSION OF CHRIST

This meditation and the next will be devoted to the passion of Christ our Lord. In the first we shall concentrate mainly on the events leading up to the crucifixion, in the second on the cross of Christ itself. It is clear that the material content of both meditations will be largely the same.

1. *The disciples in the garden of Gethsemane*

We begin at the Mount of Olives. The Lord goes into the garden as always, knowing that the traitor will look for him there. He goes himself to meet his suffering. He goes readily. "I have power to lay down my life, and I have power to take it again. No one takes it from me" (Jn 10:18), he says himself, and goes to meet his cross. Here you have a vivid description of the nature of voluntary christian renunciation. It is the freedom with which we go to meet what is really our cross.

This ready approach is the approach to the scandal of faith: it offends the disciples who love him. "You will all be scandalized in my regard this night" (Mk 14:27 Vulgate), he tells them. Evidently the course of world-history and the course of one's own life, even entered on with the wisdom of God's love, the power of his freedom, must somehow run into the scandal of faith and love. It must be evident in this way, not because it might not be otherwise, but because in the concrete God's greater choice itself so decides between two abstract possibilities that what ought not to be and in the

216

abstract would not have to be nevertheless is open to that higher, mysterious, divine "must" of which our Lord frequently speaks (Mk 8:31; 13:10; Lk 4:43; 17:25; 24:7; Jn 9:4).

This entry into the garden is the entry of the strong into its own weakness, of courage into its own impotence, of love for the Father into abandonment by God. An incomprehensible passage, but merely the logical continuation of the "emptying" (Phil 2:7), which begins at the point where God's infinite fullness of life really and truly runs out into the finiteness of the creature. In regard to all these things, we must not say simply that the finite is what it is and God has not ceased to be infinite by his assumption of the finite. If we were to divide up the hypostatic union into two natures and to make a similar division in what follows from this as the *actus secundus* of the incarnate Word, we would have understood neither the cross nor redemption through the cross. God would then still be the one absolutely untouched in himself, and mortality, futility, impotence, weakness would be on our side only, on this side of the infinite abyss between God and the creature. Where then would be the greatness of the act? How would we be redeemed?

We must really accept the paradox and the mystery, because we are redeemed only by the fact that the strong enters as himself into his own weakness, even though we also have to say that he has remained at the same time strong, absolutely transcendent in his own power and strength and bliss. And yet it is just of this God that we must say: He is here weak, he falls on his face, he loses all power, he experiences his own abandonment by himself. Only when we take the hypostatic union seriously as meaning that God himself in person has become man, when we take this tremendous truth seriously and don't reduce its meaning to the simple statement that the hypostasis of the *Logos* was the bearer of a human nature in which all the finiteness and weakness was concentrated, only when we understand in the incomprehensibility of faith that everything which occurs here happens to God himself: only then do we accept the incomprehensible, and it is this which redeems.

2. *The sin of all*

The Lord takes with him the disciples who had been present on Mount Tabor when he was acknowledged by the law and the prophets, by the Spirit breathing where he will and by the institution in which the Spirit takes concrete shape (Mt 17:1–13). These disciples of Tabor, who saw the Lord with Moses and the prophet Elijah, are to see in Gethsemane the fulfilment of the transfiguration of the law and the prophets; they are to see how the one who is faithful to the law breaks down, how God – omnipotent creator of all law – is himself conquered by sin. The new kingdom which the prophets proclaimed and the eternal nuptials for which they longed and which they foretold, these they are to see as they now really appear.

It is when sin, to to speak, gains the upper hand, when everything apparently breaks down, and in no other way that the fulfilment of the law and the prophets comes about. It is easy to say this. We can even be consoled and soothed by this sort of paradoxical statement; but in our actual life this must also be suffered, carried through. For we always think that everything in our life must be significant up to the end, since we observe God's sacred norms. In our life we are constantly expecting – perhaps under different names and labels – the coming of the kingdom, radiating power, with which we have united ourselves in our faith, in our priesthood. You need only think of the character of our normal preaching, of our normal conception in practice of the life of the Church, of the priesthood. We will never admit that the new kingdom and the eternal nuptials of God with man come about in the way we experience it in the passion. For our part, we never consider the weakness, the impotence, the forlornness of the church and ourselves as that which has to be, because this is the way in which the law and the prophets must be fulfilled.

Jesus takes with him the disciples of Tabor, those who wanted to be more courageous, ready to die, and they take refuge in sleep from the depression that comes upon them. He takes them into the garden. They are thus to be his consolers. To them – strange as it may seem – he flees when faced by his Father's chalice: to the weary, worn-out and sleepy ones, to those who cannot make any sense out of what they experience here, who no longer have any advice to give, any solution to offer. These are his companions – and this too is what we are.

Consider the agony in the garden. In the new testament it is described as perplexity, trembling, restless fear, agony, a dread stifled so to speak by death in the final tension of his forces before the decisions and catastrophes breaking in upon him. This is the baptism of which Jesus said (Lk 12:49) that he was constrained until he reached that goal. As he says, he is sorrowful, beset with sadness even unto death. Sweat falls on the ground like drops of blood. The agony he suffers is the agony before death which unjust, hateful, vile men make him suffer. Inflicted in this way with men's guilt, he experiences the sin of the world. For whenever someone is confronted with vileness, the abyss of the world is opened before him. It is not merely this particular sin, this particular, freely chosen vileness, which is involved, but the incomprehensibility of wickedness altogether, the mystery of sin.

In each particular sin we look into the face of the sin of the world as a whole and of our own sin. When Jesus thus encounters sin, he experiences the inescapable, universal dominion of sin as a whole, poisoning all dimensions of life. Thus he suffers himself the agony of the presence of sin and he suffers it in a strange identification with sinners. For the monstrous feature of this experience of sin, which directly kills in a way which can be historically felt, is the very fact that he does experience it and cannot withdraw to a zone of his own security against sinners.

If someone hates and despises others, if he inwardly rejects the wickedness of others, if he breaks away from them, dissociates himself from them, he remains in a situation where he can be saved from this pressing vileness, stifling in death; but Jesus cannot do this, for he loves men unto death. At the very point where sin fatally comes upon him, he identifies himself with those who do this to him. Up to a point, this is what constitutes the desperate inescapability, the agonising dread of his situation. He really has to accept the absurdly vile from those with whom he identifies himself in love. It is the agony of seeing the futility of his previous work, of his work altogether.

3. *Futility*

We must not think that our Lord in the passion, in his human weakness, did not fall unconditionally into the abyss of this futility: as one who hopes of course, as the one who – as he later says on the cross – places his soul in the hands of the Father (Lk 23:46). But this in no way alters the fact that he is confronted with the absolute futility of his work. We must not think that Jesus' intention of redeeming the world and establishing the new, eternal covenant of God with men through his cross, his death, giving up his body and shedding his blood, was merely a pretence; that all his quest for supporters, his preaching of the advent of the kingdom and the need of conversion, offering the prospect of a marvellous spiritual revolution in world-history, was no more than a piece of acting. On the contrary!

He was really serious about this mission to win his people, to convince men that the kingdom of God was present in his person, and therefore he felt the agony of the infinite futility of the situation, what he did, what he said, what he loved. This too is how the agony of being abandoned by God came to be. He perished in the fate of the world. We really ought to repeat here Ignatius' meditation on hell (65–72), although we cannot hold in a false, calvinistic sense that Jesus formally suffered the torment of hell. That would be heresy: for the Son suffers everything in an ultimate, all-embracing obedience. But in this way he really bears everything. Thus occurs that abandonment which – if it is not accepted, of course – we call hell: it is the best analogue to what happens here.

4. *The chalice*

In this hour of need and futility he asks that the Father's chalice to him should pass. This is the chalice of the new testament which we grasp every day. It is the chalice of which the Son said, trembling, in unutterable weakness and fear and agony: "Remove this from me" (Lk 22:42). It is too much, it is impossible. It is humanly impossible, it is sheer horror, sheer death, sheer void, sheer disaster, absolute impotence, utterly inconceivable, darkness. Three times he says the same prayer, and he flees to the sleeping disciples, says "Yes" to the incomprehensible God and to this chalice. Since he accepts it, this chalice of the terrible history of mankind becomes the chalice of the new and eternal covenant.

Then he says: "Rise, let us be going" (Mt 26:46). Impotence gives way, the miracle happens, strength flows out of the void of the heart. It is just this that is the first and truest possibility of all things in him in whom God himself descended into the lowest depths of our Gethsemane-existence, so that there is no abyss in which God, his love, his mercy, were never yet borne at the deepest level. There is no darkness in which God does not live; no void that is not filled to its depths with him; no abyss greater than the abyss of the mystery of God, who is love, none greater than the abyss of God's mercy. We are made one with this Jesus of Gethsemane.

5. *Betrayal*

Let us consider Jesus, betrayed by Judas, forsaken by his friends. There is an abandonment by men in which is revealed the abandonment which creates sin, which forsakes God. Here we may well meditate on the three powers of the soul from within. This abandonment is an outward gaze which is blind to God, where the distortion of things and personal hatred, involved in sin, become visible: as opposed to memory, this lowest point of awareness of God; as opposed to understanding, which really sees and expresses the objective structures of reality; as opposed to the will, which seeks and finds the other person in love.

All this appears in this breaking down of interpersonal relations, so that the Son is thrust into this terrible loneliness of the man who is abandoned, betrayed, rejected. In the orbit of finite, human personality, to which he is ordered anyway as a human being, he finds nothing more to hold him, to confirm him, to give him security in his existence. Here too is the picture of the abandonment of God by God, the vulnerability of his love. The last word receives no answer. In this betrayed, forsaken, isolated, useless, abandoned Christ, can be seen the image of God who is love.

6. *Profession*

Let us also consider Jesus' profession before the high priest. This Son of Man standing wretched before the religious authority which he has acknowledged as wholly competent is Christ, the judge before whom my life is decided. They say of his profession: "He has uttered blasphemy" (Mt 26:65). He is therefore condemned in the name of reason, of order, of patriotism, of good taste, of propriety, of moderation, of reverence for God. This is the Son of man, the norm of our life!

Certainly we ought to be rational, seeing and loving order in the world, loving our country; we ought to have taste and discretion, observe the proprieties, exercise moderation in our life, acknowledge God as the model of all that we are ourselves and want to be, and then to feel that we are honouring God by attaching importance to reason, order, moderation, taste, propriety. All this is true and remains so – and yet: *Ecce homo* (Jn 19:5). Here is our Lord, the norm of our life. He seems to have been condemned very rightly and very justly in the name of all those things which are always absolute standards for us.

7. *Imprisonment*

Let us consider Jesus in prison. He is alone – in the prison of my finiteness, of my solitude, of man's absolute wastedness, of death, of the helplessness of sin. In a prison which is mine and which is open: open because he descended into it. There are times when I am unwilling to believe it, and I haven't the courage to face it. The Lord constantly tells me as he told Peter in prison: "Get up, dress yourself and go" (Acts 12:8). We always think it is merely a vision made up out of our illusions and imagination. In reality the Lord has descended into all my helplessness. Therefore everything, even sin, is open: we can go into the light, into the authentic, the beautiful, the lovable, into the community and the freedom of God. For we really are liberated, released from slavery, freed for the freedom of God, freed (as Paul says in Gal 5:1) both from the law and from sin and death. For he went into the prison of finiteness, of sin and death.

8. *Rejected*

Let us consider further how Jesus is rejected by the people of God and the pagans. He is the plaything between the two: "a stumbling block to the Jews and folly to the Gentiles" (1 Cor 1:23). He is rejected by the Jews as a scandal, as something which must be rejected in the name of the God who has revealed himself, which is rejected therefore with an almost supernatural passion. He is rejected by the pagans as folly, folly that is rejected by the judgment of their wisdom and their understanding of life. There is a wisdom of the world which presumes to be more mature than the mystery of love coming before Pilate. There is a foolish wisdom which tries undecidedly to mediate and does not understand that there can be moments in human life when the sole wisdom is the folly of love which does not fear even the cross and disaster.

9. *Beaten*

Let us consider Jesus scourged and crowned with thorns. This is the first attack on the Lord's body itself, which belongs essentially to the human person. The fatal breaking down from outside now begins. The scandal of death becomes clear, because we die in suffering, assaulted from outside. What is a scandal already in regard to the bodily nature of a free, autonomous, spontaneous person, becomes so much more terrible here, because this scandal comes not purely and simply from cruel nature, but from the personal wickedness of men. This is always the case with sin. The pitiful image of the *Ecce Homo*, produced by men through their own fault, becomes for men the provocation and excuse for their contempt. Their own deed becomes the justification for their work of destruction, because they managed it; it is the blind and fatal justification that it was good because it exists. That is how sin comes about: the vileness of the world is once again justified in its own deed for its own damnation.

This scourged body, this head, becomes the image of the world as a whole, in which God wills to reveal himself: the image of the nature of sin, the scourging of God and his crowning with thorns in the suffering of the world. The body which is the church is treated in the same way by the world and by us. We look on the Lord and let Pilate tell us: *Ecce homo*. This is man, poor, thrust into death, who is God's precisely in Jesus. When we accept his grace, which is the grace of this fate and the grace of enduring this fate with Jesus, we too can see ourselves in this *Homo* and there recognise our fate and our promise.

21 THE CROSS OF CHRIST

We shall now make our second meditation on the cross of Christ.

1. *The cross – and the Jews, Hellenes and christians*

If we wanted to make the meditation with the sublime technique of St Ignatius, we would have to put before ourselves as the *compositio loci* the history of mankind with all its wickedness, its fantastic ignorance, its passion, its atrociousness. We would have to see this at all times, in all peoples, as the disgrace of all nations, as the disgrace of christians who were no better than the others. In the midst of this race of sinners, of the dying, of the afflicted, the cross of Christ rises up.

Then we might say with Paul: "The word of the cross is folly to those who are perishing, but to us who are being saved it is the power of God" (1 Cor 1:18). We would have to consider Paul's words: "But we preach Christ crucified" (1 Cor 1:23). We would have to speak almost of "the man on the gallows", who is a scandal to the Jews, folly to the gentiles; but to us who have heard the call, this Christ on the cross is the *dynamis*, the power and wisdom of God. We would have to consider what Paul means by the Jew for whom this cross is a scandal. A Jew in this sense is a man who has understood God and knows exactly what he is. He is a man who applies moral norms as if they were mathematical rules, enabling us to see precisely what is good and what is bad. If we follow these rules, we are living in friendship with God, we have understood God, God can have nothing against us, what follows must also be covered by these rules of systematic morality, everything must turn out well: at the end there cannot be someone hanging on the gallows, done to death by men and to be worshipped as God's wisdom and power. That is how judaism protests in the name of God and religion against the one who is supposed to be our wisdom and power and is nailed to the cross.

If we put aside our habits for once, if we clean out of ourselves what we learned just in this way, if we look at the religion which we really practise and don't merely talk about, do we in fact understand the wisdom and power of God, is the one hanging on the cross in fact our philosophy and power, our life's strength? Imagine that Jesus had not passed, so to speak, into a mystical-mythical darkness of the past, but that it is happening now. The police grab somebody, beat him up, strip him of his clothes, put him on the gallows, and he dies there, crying out: "My God, why hast thou forsaken me?" Could we in all seriousness fall down before him and say: *Ave crux, spes unica, hoc passionis tempore?* In the midst of my passion, does this one on the gallows reveal here the meaning of my life and give me the true philosophy of life and the true power to endure it – would we manage this? If not, is our christianity merely a package of traditions, of ingrained habits, unctuous talk?

Paul says that the Hellene must regard this cross as folly, obtuseness, stupidity, narrowness, unquestionable perversity. The man who finds joy here below in spirit and soul, body and beauty, will also see the tragic element in life, but he will not admit that this is more than something to be tacitly accepted in a life that is otherwise bright, clear, earthy, sunny. If he is told that the crucifixion is the sign of his life's meaning, he will go on to say with a shrug of his shoulders that life cannot and must not be so tasteless, so perverse, so negatively twisted. He is not going to let himself be involved in this sort of offensiveness, but will pass over the stupidity in silence and get on without more discussion to the rest of the agenda.

Paul says that we ourselves are Jews and Hellenes and remain so. Faith in the cross is something for which we must never cease to pray and to struggle, something above all which must be suffered in life itself: for it is only from this source that the true grace comes of those who are called in incomprehensible grace. To these this very cross, God's powerlessness in the world, in ourselves, in the church, becomes his strength. They will not produce statistics to show that the Roman catholic church is the largest in the world, they will not take it as proved from any sorts of institution that the church is the most brilliantly organised association which can ever be conceived in the world; in their own life too they will distrust success, suspect all experience that comes too easily without a hint of death; they will understand the apparent impotence of God's truth as the power of God, "so that no human being might boast" (1 Cor 1:29), so that every voice should be stilled, that everyone should fall down in adoration before the God who makes the true beginning of all reality at the very point where everything seems to reach its end.

In spite of their judaism and their hellenism, those who are called in the depths of their nature will see wisdom in the cross of God, will recognise that the folly of love is the meaning of the world. If they have understood this, they will not say that there is no more than this cross, but will know that this terrible, monstrous, incomprehensible thing is again embraced by the love of the God of glory. Everything else will be added to them: even joy of life, frankness, harmony with the world as that which itself has to be saved. But everything goes through this small point, which is in fact the cross of Christ: for with us everything runs out into death. The question therefore remains: are we to stick to what is passing or to death? The christian sticks to both: to the world, to God and to the folly of the cross. But since this folly is the most difficult, it is and remains also our greatest task. We need not perhaps hasten, we perhaps don't need to be anxious about it, we should only say to God: If you set up the cross in my life, where you will, when you will, I must take it from you that I am one who is called, who through your grace recognises in it God's wisdom and power. For the time being, I will act in such a way so as not on my part to prevent this chance of a grace that you must give me.

2. *The cross in the life of Jesus*

Let us consider the cross in the life of Jesus. According to Jesus' own words, it is the culmination of his mission: "Father, the hour has come; glorify thy Son" (Jn 17:1). By this he means the cross: for, lifted up on it, he is the one glorified by the Father. It is the culmination of his mission, because he says that he "came not to be served, but to serve" and – as Mt 20:28 adds – "to give his life as a ransom for many." He says of himself that he must suffer, that he must be lifted up, that he must rise from the dead (Mk 8:31). In other words, everything can be mission.

This is something that we are never wholly willing to understand. There is no situation which might not be mandate and task. A mandate is always a burden and vice-versa. Every burden, even death, is again a mission, perhaps exactly as it was with our Lord, the culmination of his mission. Ultimately, fate and men cannot touch us. For what they send us is Christ's fate and mission and mandate and task. Even at the point where we are powerless, we have done the greatest deed and fulfilled our mandate; but this very culmination of the mission in Jesus' life followed on his life's catastrophe, the failure of his mission, the abandonment by his friends, being thrust out of the nation for betraying the highest national interests. For he is betrayed by his apostles, although properly speaking he cannot be betrayed. In reality only someone who has already betrayed himself can be betrayed. Nevertheless, what is incomprehensible takes place here: men run away from him although he is the absolutely unmistakable one, completely composed, the one who has come to grips with himself, firm and clear, unconditioned, not already dialectically split. He is betrayed and he is also rejected by the community founded by God himself in the old testament, which was the church of the time before Jesus Christ. We do in fact believe – and rightly – as the content of our faith that the church which stems from the wound in the side of the one done to death on the cross and which was formed as the second Eve from the side of the second Adam cannot betray this bridegroom. This is always true, not however as a human achievement, but by the greater grace of God. The people who are actually in the church are of themselves just as wretched, as shabby, as calculating, as the leaders in the old testament who rejected the Son of Man.

It is his life's catastrophe, in so far as he is tortured to death, in so far as his love is rejected, in so far as he is forsaken by God, in so far as life is given up to death, in so far as he became sin (2 Cor 5:21), he who knew no sin. Here too we must not make distinctions too easily or too quickly in order to soften these words. We have already seen that he identifies himself with sin: for he endures guilt in his cruel death and at the same time loves his hangman. But then there is really nothing more to rely upon. Not even a protest against the people who do this to him. The cross is the culmination of his life's work. To that extent, this cross is the "Yes" to the end, to impotence, abandonment and death – and he is thus obedient, as Isaiah says of the servant of Yahweh, *quia ipse voluit* (Is 53:7); we read of him that he was obedient unto death, "even death on a cross" (Phil 2:8). It is really attested that the Lord says "Yes" to the most cruel, extreme impotence, to this fate, which is the pure contradiction of himself.

We cannot die such a death, since for us darkness, impotence, evil, doom, is something of ourselves. Up to a point we experience ourselves in these things and not the merely senseless contradiction of ourselves. We have already in ourselves the "No" of death. But with him it was different. Therefore all that comes upon him approaches him so to speak as the absolutely other, as a contradiction, as incompatible with him. It invades him as that which comes completely from outside.

This is not to deny that he was inwardly mortal. But this inward mortality is something he has accepted and therefore it is an unutterable "Yes" that stands behind the radical contradiction in his life in order to hold this contradiction in itself, in order to find a place for it. At the same time it is not denied that the person who is caught and overwhelmed is the one who of himself could assume that he was simply the pure, absolute "No" to that which comes upon him.

Jesus says "Yes" to the end, to impotence, abandonment and death. He really is the one who is obedient. The culmination of Jesus' moral act is love for the incomprehensible God, falling into his consuming judgment. In the epistle to the Hebrews (10:31) we read that it is a fearful thing to fall into the hands of the living God. He who became sin for us falls into those hands and says: "Into thy hands I commit my spirit" (Lk 23:46). With eyes darkened by blood and the shadow of death, he looks towards the thief and says: "Today you will be with me in Paradise" (Lk 23:43). In the old testament, in the psalms (Ps 6:6), we pray: *In inferno autem quis confitebitur tibi?* This theology of death as the theology of the poor man still remains true.

There is only one who can praise God as he falls into the abyss of death and that is Christ our Lord; all the others can do this only in him. This moral act of Jesus is that of the Son in the infinite dignity and depth of his being. Here too if we really want to understand the theology of the hypostatic union, we would not have to think simply of this *dignificatio ratione naturae* in a purely static, juridical sense. However closely the divine and the human reality are united as *symphytos* in the incarnate *Logos*, this very distinction between his humanity and his actual fate is created by being accepted, made known, as the reality of the *Logos* himself (for the reality of the *Logos* himself proceeds from the depths of God's created power). It is really and truly his, so that what happens here is the fate of the *Logos* himself. If God declares himself into the void of creatureliness, there arises not only man, but the crucified one and his fate.

3. *The universal significance of the cross*

Let us consider the cosmic, redemptive-historical, universal significance of the cross and death of our Lord. This cross is the revelation of sin. Sin is in the world in such a way that this is what happens when the *Logos* himself comes into his own. It is here that we can first of all consider the insane blindness of sin. On the cross we observe the hatred – which can be inflamed by love – and the hopelessness of sin. This is sin, this is my sin too – as what has happened, as a permanent, intrinsic possibility for me.

What is said in Hebrews 6:6 holds for us: "They crucify the Son of God and hold him up to contempt." In face of this revelation of our sin, we must say with Paul (Gal 2:20): "He loved me and gave himself for me". Whether we are holy or not, whether we have sinned much or little, what happened there was necessary for us. This cosmic, universal significance of the cross and death lies in the fact that it is the culmination of God's love. "God so loved the world that he gave his only Son, that whoever believes in him should not perish but have eternal life" (John 3:16). Here we must consider what Paul (Rom 5:8) says, "while we

were yet sinners Christ died for us," and what John
(31:1) says of Jesus, "he loved them to the end," even
to the cross. This cross, which thus becomes the revelation of sin and the revelation of God's love, as the unity
of both is then the redemption of the world from death
and sin. "Where sin increased, grace abounded all the
more" (Rom 5:20). What Paul says (Rom 11:32) remains true: "God has consigned all men to disobedi-
ence, that he may have mercy upon all." Here and only
here can we begin to understand also the real meaning
of devotion to the sacred heart. The heart as the centre
of Christ himself, pierced by sin and thus – so to speak
– running out into futility, into death, and therefore
redemptive.

4. *The cross of Christ in my life*
What does the cross of Christ mean in my life? First of
all we must never forget that the christian may not be
more self-pitying in his own life than the pagans who
do not know or do not seem to know God. The common
sense of the realistic, brave man, courage in face of
pain, taking renunciation for granted, not indulging in
lamentations and not being self-important; calm, silent,
resigned bravery in regard to life: all these things,
which the pagans sometimes exemplify better, are also
part of the christian life. Because he understands his
relationship to the cross in the light of his faith in the
cross of Christ, this does not mean that the christian
must be plaintive and cowardly about it. The fact that
our life is a participation in the life of Christ does not
give us any right to cowardliness and self-pity: we
should be just as brave, generous, serious and un-
perturbed as a person who knows nothing of the cross.

Nor does the cross of Christ in our life mean that we have to indulge in a frenzy of sacrifice and renunciation.

There is anyway a degree of suffering and involvement in death which simply cannot be mastered by a bravery that is wholly of this world, because death overpowers man and not man death, since it is in death – otherwise death would not be death – that he is deprived of that very autonomous strength in which and through which he might be brave. This does not mean that those who do not believe in Christ or do not seem to know about him cannot die the death of Christ, if obediently and silently in a final grasp of the meaning of their life they accept death and all its futility. For then – whatever further distinctions theologians may adduce – they have died the death which man dies in Christ, a redeeming death. They have believed and loved, they have died in Christ and in his death. We, who know expressly what happens or can happen in the depth of our nature, should be particularly aware of this.

In the life of the christian the cross of Christ should mean a continual act of faith and hopeful endurance, as Paul (1 Thess 1:3) says. Involved in this are christian asceticism and the evangelical counsels, the third degree of humility, a ready faith and the exercise of the will to believe, the acceptance of the cross in our own lives just as it happens and even when it comes overpoweringly in death. As priests particularly we must see the sufferings of Christ (Col 1:24) as suffering for the body of Christ, which is the church. There is really nothing more to be said about this, but we must ask ourselves constantly whether we are really prepared to assume the signs of Christ's death and recognise these as signs of election or whether in the depth of our existence we still flee from the cross of Christ or – to put it more modestly – whether we at least allow ourselves to be overtaken by it or not.

Finally, is all this reflection once again to end quite calmly, humbly, in the question: Where then do I find my cross today, not tomorrow or the day after tomorrow? If as a priest you have to deal with men, you will learn what you could learn from your own experience, if you would take the trouble to do so, that people talk about love of the cross but simply do not recognise as such the cross that they are meant to accept and therefore properly speaking the whole man is somehow inwardly neurotically twisted. He protests against a thousand things in life and will not accept them, will not come to terms with them, will not let them rise to the surface, denies them, thinks that he cannot bear them. These things of course are not called the cross of Christ. Our spiritual jargon does not penetrate so far into the reality of our life. That is why we often fail to recognise where the real cross of Christ is now in our life. But perhaps we might ask God for the grace to persevere for the few hours of our life under the cross of Christ, under the tree of the knowledge of good and evil, under the tree of life, until we too can return our poor souls into the hands of God: crucified and thus liberated for eternal life.

22 THE RISEN ONE

Christian life as a whole is always and everywhere sustained by the death and resurrection of our Lord. His grace is always the grace of the crucified and risen one. It lives in us always as a whole, even though its history consists of successive phases in which we are led bit by bit through the reality which it contains in germ and in power.

We can make only one meditation on the risen and exalted Christ. We must be clear from the beginning that death, resurrection, ascension, are *one* event, phases of one event which itself brings these phases together into an inner unity. The evangelist Luke sums up these phases when he says: "Was it not necessary that the Christ should suffer these things and enter into his glory?" (Lk 24:26). The apostle Paul likewise sums up death and resurrection as one event in the life of Jesus: "He was put to death for our trespasses and raised for our justification" (Rom 4:25). That is why Paul can assign the *one* saving deed of Christ in our regard to these two factors of death and resurrection. The same unity of the two phases might be considered in the light of the concept of sacrifice. The accepted sacrifice is in fact the risen Lord and this sacrifice is consummated only by being accepted by God. This means: the resurrection and exaltation of the Lord.

1. *The risen victor*
Christ is the risen victor. In the Easter liturgy he is

addressed: *Tu nobis, victor rex, miserere.* The death that we feel within ourselves is already overcome in him. The world, its narrowness and wickedness, is overcome. The love of the Father, of the incomprehensible God, is for him the radiant present, and the whole, *one* reality of the man Jesus is taken up into this conquest of death. We cannot make a distinction here between transfiguration of the body and that of the soul. Man is originally one and these elements, called body and soul, are in fact elements of this one reality. Neither can be conceived as for itself alone without the knowledge of one leading to the other and this other being drawn into the conception of the one. So there is also in the one man Jesus Christ, composed of body and soul, the perfection of the whole man.

2. *The exalted Lord*

Paul says (1 Cor 10:11) that the end of time has come. We live today at a time which seems to offer – and up to a point really does offer extraordinarily broad horizons of the future. We are experiencing – so to speak – a sudden acceleration of the evolution of mankind. There is no doubt that in our brief lifetime we have in a certain sense experienced greater variety in new inventions, in new events, in quite different prospects, than people did in former times – say, perhaps, a hundred years ago. This is why modern man thinks that everything is really beginning now for the first time. Space is being conquered; the innermost core of physical reality is being penetrated; inventions are planned gradually, they do not occur by chance; all this is organised. Man lives in a higher dimension, he lives more intensely, and – at least apparently – he is open to unforeseeable prospects. All the resources of the great nations are concentrated on these goals and people have the impression that they are living now only for the sake of a greater future.

This is all very fine, but it remains true that we have reached the end of the great world-epochs. Why? Because Jesus Christ is exalted to the right hand of the Father. He, the God-man, in his divine-human reality, has already superseded all possibilities open to man as man, not by arbitrarily setting an end to things from outside, but because he has already surpassed these human possibilities by entering into God's infinity.

Man's goal is the absolute infinity of God, which is not pieced together out of the finitenesses of this world. *This* infinity already exists in Jesus Christ. Since Jesus Christ possesses this infinity of God, man in him – in this humanity – is transfigured in every dimension. Thus man is already carried beyond himself into God: it is really true that he is infinitely more than a man. This man and these possibilities of infinite fullness are in fact already attained in man as such, in the God-man who is mediator between mankind and God. Thus the end is already present. This end, already existing, can only be filled out; for the rest, it can be pervaded by the reality of the world and by humanity. It cannot be superseded and surpassed, but only carried on to the last moment, which is already now.

This means then that the absolute future has already arrived: for us indeed it is still only present in faith and veiled, but truly present. The significance of this intramundane futurity and this future-oriented historical dynamism of mankind, towards the future, already present, of the infinite God, is something that need not be considered here. So far as nature has any importance at all for supernature – and this it undoubtedly has, even as *potentia oboedientialis* – this evolution of the world and mankind, which is only just beginning, certainly possesses a positive meaning for the filling out of the supernatural, divine future which has already arrived. How this can be conceived, is a question we may leave aside; in any case this whole future, which man lines up for himself, plans, and for which he mobilises all the resources of the world and of his own mind, in each individual constantly goes through the zero point of death.

It reaches the infinite future, which has already arrived, which is God himself, only through this door and not otherwise. Therefore all human future, as created by man, remains involved in the law of death and is already gloriously surpassed by Jesus Christ our Lord. However splendidly we can conceive and plan it, we see only too clearly how this human evolution always remains in the grip of the existential of mankind's historical beginning, for sin and death; we see that these basic structures of mankind as historically constituted are not abolished, not really eliminated, through its evolution, but become so much more obvious. No matter how splendid is the reality and promise of human evolution, it is clear that man is not really made happier thereby, not further moved away from death and futility, but in all this unforeseeable evolution remains in the grip of these powers of the still continuing aeons of sin, of the law, of death, of pain, of futility.

The message of christianity, of the exalted Lord, is then in fact the only really adequate and absolute

241

explanation: for now, when we see the risen one, it is possible to say that the world is already in order at a deeper level than we can yet reach. But we cannot simply leave it at that.

Think of all the horror of the world's history, of all the pain, all the despair, all the misery, all the outrages still being perpetrated by men, all the frenzied rebellion of mankind, its stupidity, its continual entanglement in its own plans; think if you like of all the concentration camps that once existed and perhaps still exist, of these heaped-up corpses, with all the terrible things that never cease to happen.

Now as christians, looking on Jesus Christ with the eyes of faith, we can say that the world at its roots is already in order. He is the living centre of the world. He is its heart. He knows that he has prevailed, in a way he feels it, he alone really understands from experience what is the ultimate and proper meaning of the world. For we must always remind ourselves that the exalted Lord, risen above all the heavens and sitting at the right hand of the Father, is not thereby cut off from the world, has not gone out of it, but is all the more deeply implanted into the heart of the world. Everything is already in him and he is in all things: in the church, in the sacrament, more than ever in the world; for through death we reach as it were the deepest level of the world, the heart of the world, the sources of all streams which flow through world-history over the surface of our outward lives. He who descended into the heart of the world in death did not abandon the world through his resurrection; but through his resurrection it is finally revealed that he remains the innermost centre of all reality and history as united with God, as its transfiguring, redeeming blessedness.

Our ordinary experience of world-history, of actualisation of the existentials already planted at the roots and the beginning of world-history, is of the secondary; our contact is with what is already abolished in its deepest roots, with the merely provisional, with the flow of a stream of sin, of folly, of vileness, already drained out from its primary sources and only flowing still through the valleys of our time just at the points where we carry on our outward life.

The exalted Lord is Lord of the world, he is on the throne of the Father. This sort of expression, *sede a dextris meis*, is obviously metaphorical. What a tremendous thing however it is to say as the truth of the world and of our existence that he ascended and sits at the right hand of God the Father almighty. In former times it was impossible to realise what this means, because in fact the older metaphysics which served as background for this statement remained more or less formal and abstract. But think of the God of these worlds, as we know them now, with their milliards of light years: this God, for whom these worlds, which we are gradually coming to know, are also only a drop in the ocean; this God whom we know and experience as the creator of nature and of world-history, although through a crushing incomprehensibility and diversity of creation, since we no longer survey history as men did in former times, thinking that they could see what God had set up in the world, thinking they knew the *machina mundi*. Suarez still has the same idea: once you have gone upwards across a couple of Aristotelian terrestrial spheres, you soon arrive at the empyrean heaven. There then we can see the risen, transfigured man Jesus sitting, as *ascendens super omnes coelos*.

How incomprehensible and inconceivable all that we confess here has become in the meantime. In this way this truth has only become greater and more tremendous. Man as we know him, whose dimensions we seem to estimate, in sorrow, love, hope and joy, is really the one who will be with God for all eternity, so that the theology of eternity as a theology of God will throughout eternity be an anthropology: we shall be eternally unable to speak adequately of God unless we say that he is man.

This is really an improbable apotheosis of man. How must we really conceive and understand man? How would we have to live our own life if we were to regard and perceive man as the eternal transfigured self-utterance of God, so that in a way he understands men and man can understand himself only in God, so that this understanding of God in the God-man is really a factor in the self-understanding of man. Since we are brothers of this God-man, since it is this man in one humanity, it remains eternally true that we understand even ourselves only when we understand ourselves as truly – not in a superficial sense, but in the most radical, metaphysical sense – the brothers of this God-man. We have grasped the truth about ourselves only when we have, so to speak, finally abandoned ourselves, seized on God and there completely found ourselves. This is what it means when we say that the exalted Jesus is on the right hand of God and as such naturally also the innermost reason of our existence.

Think too in this connection of the heavenly sacrifice. What you are doing as a priest at mass is to celebrate a cosmic liturgy; or, better, this liturgy of the church, which mirrors and proclaims in space and time the eternal, infinite, cosmic liturgy of the exalted Lord on the right hand of God, is an efficacious sign of this divine liturgy. It is a sign which raises this space of ours, our time, our life, up into the liturgy of eternity, in which the creature is really and truly placed in adoration before the infinite God, but in such a way that it is aware at the same time that its own life is the life of God himself. What Paul says then (1 Cor 15:28), *Deus omnia in omnibus*, is already established and finally assured by the exalted Lord.

3. *The christian's courage for victory*

This exalted Lord is still remote, the one whom we believe, whose return, the consummation of his unique coming in the flesh, we are still expecting. We are witnesses for him as the one who has come and who is to come; we proclaim his coming in this "prognostic sign" of the mass, so that we really live this eschatology, waiting for the Lord like patient servants in the night with the lamp of faith, of hope and love. Bearing everything, enduring the world's noise, the evolution of the world, in patience, even getting a thrill out of our part in all this and sharing the experience, we nevertheless know that our future is the advent of God, which has already begun and is already present in the depth of our life in what we call the spirit of the glorified Lord.

All this is the true, real future. This is the ultimate source of the christian's courage for victory. "Be of good cheer, I have overcome the world" (Jn 16:33). "In the world you have tribulation": that is, those

245

birth-pangs and growing pains in which the true reality of this world must break out from the depths to shape and form the world. Christ as Son is over the house and we are his house, says the epistle to the Hebrews (3:6), "if we hold fast our confidence and pride in our hope." Thence stems our confidence, thence we can come with this proud assurance to the throne of grace. In virtue of the blood of Jesus, says the epistle to the Hebrews (10:19), we have the confidence to enter the sanctuary. When we simply say "dear God" and are not thinking anthropomorphically in this respect, we are already saying to the incomprehensible one the tremendous word: Father. We can say this only because we can enter with the risen Christ, through his death, into the sanctuary of God. The exhortation of the epistle to the Hebrews therefore holds for us: Do not throw away your confidence (10:35).

We must constantly remind ourselves that love and mercy are final, that love will never again be vanquished. For God's sake don't let us preach christianity as if God had left man his freedom, left the decision to him, had merely offered him in friendliness and benevolence the opportunity to make a right decision and nothing more. This existential, equitable dualism, which we often preach and in our own asceticism mostly observe, is basically false. Of course, as individuals in actual situations, we cannot and may not take it as certain that we are saved. We must remember that we are still on the way, that we must work out our salvation "in fear and trembling" (Phil 2:2). But world-history is not a pair of scales which God has in his hands and where we distribute the weights on both sides: it is a history already decided in its totality

246

through God's own act. His love has finally prevailed. For the whole of world-history God's judgment is one of love and mercy.

We can really say with St Paul: "Neither death nor life, nor angels, nor principalities, nor things present, nor things to come, nor powers, nor height, nor depth, nor anything else in all creation, will be able to separate us from the love of God in Christ Jesus our Lord" (Rom 8:38–39). We must believe in the efficacious grace of God and not merely in sufficient grace. We have a duty to hope absolutely that God has had mercy on us in Christ and that we have part forever in that which has been set right by what Christ, crucified and risen, has done. We share in the superiority of Christ, risen to new and eternal life and brought into heaven, because we are placed with him in heaven (Eph 2:6): that is, we have gone beyond all things, beyond the world, beyond the powers of world-history, beyond sin, beyond the burden of the flesh, beyond death. As christians, we are the new people, the soul of the world. For our sake, says the *Epistle to Diognetus*, the world subsists. Justin writes to the emperor that christians more than all other men are his fellow-workers and fellow-warriors for world-peace.

We need not adopt without more ado the ideology of the "better world", since the world must sustain the death of Christ and the futility of his cross, since we christians too have no recipes to render superfluous dying, misery, poverty, the running around in circles that continues throughout world-history. However good the recipes we have for this life, we should not promise people that we have the means of turning this world at once into God's paradise. People don't really want to hear this at all, because deep down they don't believe it anyway.

Death and futility are there and man knows it; and all the stir caused by modern ideologies of the future is merely a token of this final insecurity. Thus we can, may and must tell people to trust Christ who conquers the world. The true, the only salvation of the whole world has already come to pass: a man from this world, taking it with him, penetrating it for the first time, has really found his way through it to the absolute God. The christian's courage for victory is of course the impotence of the cross: for Christ conquered first on the cross. We are those who see the world's fate composedly, quietly, naturally, calmly, take it on ourselves and know that there is one who has conquered, and that this is our Lord Jesus Christ.

23 SPIRIT, CHURCH, MARY

1. *The Spirit*

The outpouring of the Spirit and the founding of the church are essential factors in the consummation of the redemptive-historical event of Jesus Christ. Since he is the exalted Lord, he pours out the Spirit over all flesh and by so doing proves himself to be the risen one and exalted to the right hand of God. The realisation of this Spirit is the church. We, who believe in him and are established in him as our salvation in living and in dying, are born of water and Spirit, from the Spirit and through the sacrament, in fact through the church. Hence Spirit and church necessarily belong together.

This idea is found throughout the new testament. The spring of water (Jn 4:14), welling up to eternal life, is notably a statement about the Spirit as living water, but points nevertheless to baptism (Jn 19:34). So too his flesh is the bread of life (Jn 6:41–65), but at the same time we are told: "The words I have spoken are spirit." If the living waters, the streams of the Spirit, flow from Christ's side (Jn 7:37–38), the same connection between the flesh and the Spirit, the sacramental sign and the inward grace, the historicity of the church and her fullness of the Spirit, are constantly present. These two things belong necessarily together, just as blood and water flowed from the pierced side of the saviour on the cross, so that we may recognise that he is the source of the Spirit. Jesus came through the water, the blood and the Spirit (1 Jn 5:6–8) and, when we look to the centre of our salvation, we read in the Book of Revelation (1:7): "Every eye will see him, everyone who pierced him"; and the lamb that was slaughtered leads them to the springs of living water (Rev 7:17). Spirit and church belong together.

In our reflexions on the gift of salvation, which is the Spirit, we should first of all remember that we have this Spirit. In the last resort, this is a reality of which faith tells us. Nevertheless, Spirit and experience merge into one another much more than is suggested in a number of theories of the spiritual life. We have this Spirit, we live by him, we experience his dynamism, although we cannot perhaps distinguish it unequivocally from the rest of our experience. As spirit, we are always transcendent, open to infinite reality. There is no internal limit to the Spirit, enclosing him as it were inwardly into a finite space, and to this extent the experience of spiritual transcendence, of the essential spiritual nature of man, and the experience of grace – which certainly exists if we really think correctly, metaphysically and theologically – are naturally not easy to distinguish from one another.

The dynamism of our transcendence as such and that divine dynamism which seizes on and transcends and elevates the natural, involved as they are in our mental life as a whole, cannot easily be demarcated from one another. This presumably cannot be done in a reflexion as such. But once we know that the Spirit of God really lives in us through baptism, through justification, in love, then it becomes clear that we experience this in the ultimate depths of our mental life: hunger for God, our absolute and infinite claims, this longing for eternal life, this final protest against death which rises from the depth of our supernaturally elevated life, this courage of indifference, of dissociation from the finite good, since it can never be identified with what is absolutely necessary for the fulfilment of our nature.

In short, when the christian speaks of God's grace in connection with his experience and practice of the christian life, he may and must understand and interpret this as experience of the supernatural, of the grace of the holy Spirit of God himself drawing him into the inner divine life. What else can it mean when Paul says that we not only live in the Spirit but are to walk in the Spirit (Rom 8:4)? What can it mean that the Holy Spirit cries out in us with unspeakable sighs (Rom 8:26)? That we should manifest the *dynamis* and *energeia* of the Spirit even in our apostolic life (2 Cor 12:12)? That we are really consoled (Phil 1:19)? That we have confidence in the Holy Spirit (Gal 5:5)?

When we divide up these things – which are completely within the sphere of our mental life – into something which is purely human in its own sphere of experience and the same thing elevated ontologically at a point where we no longer rightly know what is the good of it all, we tear apart the very unity of the supernatural mental life in the Spirit of God. We then turn what we are doing as persons into a supremely uninteresting, toilsome, poverty-stricken, merely human affair and maintain that the Spirit of God is not present where we are as persons: for the reality of spiritual personality lies in what we do, what we bring about in freedom, what we long for – our fear, our love, our hope, our bliss, our free decision, our loyalty – these are not marginal phenomena, as if the essential, real, true element of the spiritual person were something dead, stale, without self-awareness. No: if the person is and comes to be in his substantial reality where he leads his life, and if that reality is not merely shaped and formed by what is called "grace" (ie in nominalist terms) but rather if true personal life is really shaped and formed by the Spirit, then the spiritual reality of the divine Spirit as the deifying of our nature may indeed be beyond our power subsequently to distinguish from our nature as such, but cannot be something merely entitatively outside consciousness.

We have the Holy Spirit and we can say that, whenever we deny ourselves in faith and hope and love and reach out beyond finite reality in true longing and in true courage, whenever we practise indifference and not only theoretically but in virtue of the decision of our own innermost nature, whenever we continue to believe in the light amid the darkness of this world, whenever we endure the cross of Christ, what we are living and experiencing is the veritable life of the Holy Spirit. Of ourselves perhaps we cannot estimate the range of this infinite, divine, powerful dynamism of our spiritual life, we cannot perhaps suspect that what is happening and what is really seeking to transcend the finite extends into the innermost unrelatedness of God and reaches its goal only when we know God face to face and know him as we are known. But this we know through faith. Our own experience is interpreted, elucidated, explained more precisely, through this faith. On the other hand however faith, this innermost spiritual-personal experience reaching out into the infinite, also interprets and elucidates what we learn in faith about our supernatural, divine engracing, about our possession of the Spirit. If we were to work here in a too positivistic-extrinsicist way, people of today would at least get the impression that we were telling them about some mysterious affair which is possibly quite clear and right, but with which they have nothing to do in their actual lives.

It is clear in the *Exercises* how Ignatius really thinks and what his theology is in regard to the divine Spirit. He speaks of God really directly dealing with his creature. Where do we find anything like this in our ordinary moral theology? He speaks of God himself dealing directly with his creature, with individuals seeking to understand correctly the times of election and to interpret correctly the stirrings of the divine Spirit which they experience; he speaks of God declaring his will to the creature, telling it something that the creature could not adequately and unequivocally deduce from the abstract norms of moral theology – even from those taught by the church.

Ignatius is a man of the Spirit and an existentialist in the best sense. His is not a situation-ethic, for he knows that all this movement of the Spirit is in accordance with the universal norms of the natural and super-natural moral law and that he moves man *intra limites sanctae matris ecclesiae*. But he is and remains a really modern existentialist, since he knows that the indivi-dual person experiences a direct movement on the part of the living God which he cannot possibly deny to be really entitatively supernatural or to be more than the sort of movement which might arise out of our nature or be caused by our situation. On the contrary, Igna-tius is certain that the individual human being has to deal with the living God in a supremely personal and direct way. This means that he lives and acts and feels himself driven by the true Spirit of God. If you relate all this to Ignatius' trinitarian mysticism, it becomes much clearer.

We have the Holy Spirit. We know him, we feel invigorated by him, consoled, encouraged to pray, in him we call on God himself as he really is. We know that we are already raised to eternal life and that what we do in the present time is the coming to be of an infinite, blessed possession of the Spirit for eternity. And yet we have to admit that it does not seem as if we have this Spirit, who is given to us for our salvation and is experienced. Our experience seems rather to be that we are without the Spirit, that we are forsaken by God, that we are poor, impotent, cowardly, fearing death, earthly minded, unable to see beyond the things of this world, identifying ourselves with finite goods in such a way as to make it difficult to attain indifference and the third degree of humility, to acquire a real love of the cross. This apparent experience of spiritlessness, of the Spirit's absence, of the silence of God, of the apparent powerlessness of his grace, is of course something that partly belongs to our creaturely-pilgrim situation, to the way in which the Spirit is now given, to faith and not to vision.

This experience moreover is also a consequence of the particular, very primitive stage of development of our spiritual life, and finally also a part of our guilt, or even a part of the task of enduring the spiritlessness and godlessness of our own time and generation, our task as christians and as priests. Perhaps there is in fact a situation in time, which is mysterious and supernatural also, of man's relationship to God and his Spirit. Certainly as christians we cannot say with some aphorism-

producing philosophers that the period of God's absence
has dawned in the sense that Christ's final and definitive meaning for salvation is abolished. But within this
permanent eschatological situation of the outpouring
of the Spirit, of the definitive acceptance of the world,
of really victorious grace, both in the life of individuals
– even in the life of the saints – and in the history of the
church and the world, there can perhaps be periods
when God's silence is a mark of the age.

Why should not something like this be possible? Why
should there be only in the history of nature or in the
secular history of ideas something like a kind of style of
the age to which the most varied things are subject
within that period, in spite of their very great diversity?
It is possible to conceive something like this in the
supernatural phases of salvation history as well, since
here too God guides not only individual human beings
but also history as a whole in good times and bad; it
was so in the life of our Lord himself, at one time
exultant in his praise of the Father and at another time
prostrate, sweating blood and begging God to let the
chalice pass. Perhaps a meditation of this kind on what
we should or should not expect and demand in our age
of the church would be quite opportune and important.
The free, sovereign rule of the Spirit of God – who is
given to us, whom we possess, who can however give
himself to us in completely different ways, in the experience of our power and in the experience of our powerlessness – is exercised as if the Spirit were far away.

If we complain too much about the lack of a genuine
enthusiasm, of a magnificent and glorious outburst of
the Spirit in the depth of our own life, in our priestly
activity and in the church, then we must ask ourselves

whether it is through our sin and cowardice that we fail to give scope to this Spirit who certainly would want to breathe also in our narrow ways. We must ask ourselves whether we are perhaps seeking him in the wrong place. We could certainly experience him as the divine Spirit of consolation, of confidence and of strength, but we are looking in the wrong place. Why should he show himself in power only when we are powerful? Why should he show himself as divine joy only when we are rejoicing? Why not also in our sadness? Why should we not be able to experience in our very sadness a deep, ultimate and ineffable sense of being consoled and sheltered? Why should not the experience of our need, of our dread, of our restricted knowledge, be the point at which we see that none of these things matter?

We are sheltered in God and in his love, and our ignorance and incapacity to keep going are happily and peacefully dissolved in the love of God. All this and other things we have to know and experience in order to discover the Holy Spirit as the Spirit ruling in our hearts, so long as we are aiming at true indifference, rising above the attitude of men of the second class, and not trying to dictate to the Spirit when and where he should permit himself to be experienced. Whenever we have the courage to seek him in all things, as Ignatius would say (236), we shall certainly find him very often and always be able to find him somewhere.

2. *The church*

Let us look at the church from this standpoint. We should love her. We serve her as priests. She is the efficacious primal sacrament of divine grace for us and for the world. By serving her officially we realise this primal sacrament in the situation of our time and in the circumstances of the lives of the men to whom we are sent. By really living christianity ourselves, in faith, hope and love, we make our life a part of the church herself, which, as Vatican I says, through her inexhaustible fruitfulness in all that is good and holy is in terms of fundamental theology proof of her divine mission. Through our priestly life we bear testimony – in this modern sense of testimony – to the church as divinely instituted. It is right then to give her true love. But here we must be unemotional, truthful and theologically exact.

We use expressions like *credere deum, credere deo*, and *credere in deum*, and mean by this that faith does not consist merely in holding a proposition about God's existence. We say *credere deum* and *credere deo*: we not only believe God as the guarantor of certain propositions, but in faith as a specifically supernatural act sustained by the holy Spirit of God. Above and through all theoretical propositions of faith, there is established an immediate personal relationship to the reality of God; for in faith the very object of faith, namely God, becomes its inner principle and is then called the grace of faith, so that he through whom we believe and he whom we believe are absolutely one and the same. *Credere in deum*: because he has imparted himself to us in his divine life, divinising us in the *participatio divinae naturae*, which is a reality of faith itself, given in advance of our experience of faith, we achieve this act of faith in God and receive an immediate personal relationship to him.

We cannot believe in the church in this sense or love her in this sense. She is not a real person, but a community of people. In so far as we have to distinguish her as a social structure from the people who form the community, she is an object of faith, so that we can use the expression *credo ecclesiam*, but she is not a reality to which we can give our hearts in the same sense as we love real human beings and most of all God. This is not merely a subtle theoretical distinction which has nothing to do with reality. No: when as priests we increasingly experience the church as she is, then we begin to see that this attitude to the church, personifying her, conceiving her in a beautiful though naïve sense as a person, is not possible in the long run.

Of course we love the church. Of course we love, esteem, revere those who represent the church as her ministers and we obey them. But they are nevertheless finite human beings protected by the Spirit of God against a fundamental lapse from truth and generally (although we do not know this in regard to individuals) kept by God's grace from failing in truth; but what we experience in ourselves we also experience to an increasing extent in regard to those who represent the church. Why shouldn't we have this experience? Why should we be surprised by it? An experience of this kind is not a reason for bitterness, for malicious criticism, for remaining aloof: it is an experience we can admit calmly and objectively.

The church we serve, for which we venture our life, for which we wear ourselves out is the pilgrim church, the church of sinners, the church which must be protected and preserved each day through a fresh and unparalleled miracle of grace in God's truth, love and grace. Only by seeing her in this way can we love her rightly. If she were to appear to us plainly and undifferentiated, as the absolute realisation of all our wishes, our longings, with everything as we would want it, there could not be, as there should be, this genuine, sacrificial, humbly enduring love for the church. The church would then be no more than a name for our own egoism. The church would be the projection and objectivation of what we ourselves are, what we feel and think, and not the demand for what God wants of us.

True love for the church is a love coming from the Holy Spirit, as grace of faith in the inner reality of the church which cannot be perceived directly or empirically. Of course, even the external, historical and present-day appearance of the church provides an argument in fundamental theology, a *ratio credibilitatis et credentitatis*; but it does not provide a reason for faith, only a motive of credibility and of the duty of faith – which is something quite different. We believe the church because we believe in God and, for this faith in God revealing himself through the church and in the church, the church can never be the ground of faith, but at best a ground of the credibility of God's message.

These distinctions are becoming much more important today than in former times, because we can no longer produce a spontaneous enthusiasm for the church and there is no reason for torturing ourselves to produce this when we don't feel like it. Nevertheless the church is really an instance of the application of such a selfless, enduring, humble, detached love, particularly for us who want to be and ought be wholeheartedly her priests. But we can nevertheless see the church as the community of pilgrims going forward in faith, kept together by God's grace. What we experience in ourselves, our distress, our ignorance, our lack of solutions, we can and may experience in a similar way in the church. The fact that these people, in spite of their sinfulness, in spite of their groping in darkness, nevertheless love God, trust in God, this in a way is what makes the church the church. For if she were merely a magnificent, world-wide, elaborately constructed apparatus and in this sense a *societas perfecta*, she would not be the church. The most decisive factor in the church is and remains her Holy Spirit, who is poured out in the members of the church as faith, hope and love. All ministries and mandates exist only to serve this Spirit of the church of men. Where this takes place – this bearing the cross, this love of neighbour, this hope, this profession of faith in God the incomprehensible, in Jesus Christ crucified – there occurs what is ultimate and most decisive in the church as such.

This love obviously means not only a love for the spirit of the church, but a sustaining, humble love for the body of the church, even a love for the weakness of the church. If we were to let ourselves become bitter as a result of our experience of this church, if we were to withdraw into a church of abstract unhistorical ideals, we should also have betrayed the true Spirit of the church: for he is precisely a Spirit who comes with water and with blood, the sacrifice and the flesh of Jesus Christ, and with the flesh of the crucified, the weak Christ. He is a Spirit who wants to gain the victory and to be powerful in our own weakness, therefore too in the weakness of the church. But this very fact requires of us love for the actual living church, while also requiring us simply not to act as if everything were glorious and splendid, as if the church in time were already absolutely identified with the eternal kingdom of God. It is not. In the church we need not and should not share in this cult (nor in regard to persons). These are not typical manifestations of the church and her Spirit: manifestations which can be explained in the light of modern mass conditions, but are not for that reason worthy of praise, nor are we for that reason to imitate and take part in them.

In a meditation like this we might ask ourselves some questions. How do I react as a priest to the church, to the human element in the church? How do I pray for the church? Do I trust her Spirit? Have I the right understanding of *sentire cum ecclesia*, so that I do not simply identify my taste, my peculiarities, perhaps even my divine charism, with the charisms of the church? Do I really put into practice the idea of *sentire cum ecclesia* and for that very reason feel a proper, independent responsibility for the church, for her true spirit and her true pastoral concern, and just because of this responsibility can nevertheless accept everything from the church, but not everything from every sort of person in the church, as flesh and spirit of the church?

There are also cryptogamic heresies in the church, or tendencies to heresy, and these may well be fostered up to a point by those who exercise authority in the church. If this cannot be denied of the church in former times, if it can be said today that popes failed in the past and did not recognise the signs of the times, why should not similar things exist also in the church today? Of course, neither God nor history ever give us the pleasure of seeing exactly the same mistakes made a second time. For this history is too much of a once and for all factor, but – *mutatis mutandis* – a great deal is possible in the church which is certainly not in accordance in the last resort with the rule of the Spirit of God and the Spirit of the church. "Do not be conformed to this world" (Rom 12:2) is a principle that holds here too, since the church also is constantly involved in the world as long as we sinners belong to her.

The priest serves the church, he loves her, he believes her, he sustains her and her burden. He knows that he himself is part of the burden of the church, because – however hard he tries – he contributes in his own life to what we might call the unsightliness of the pilgrim church, to the fact that she simply is not what she might be, the "sign raised up for the nations". He professes his faith in her, he knows that he has to represent her, he is ready to bear all the restrictions in which the priest is involved in his duty of representing the church and not to build up a private life as a sort of private reserve to enter after office-hours are over, where he can take off his coat and breathe again, where he can be himself.

Being ordained, we are most ourselves when we are being used up in the service of the church, of her gospel, of Jesus Christ and of God. There we really become aware of ourselves and only there: otherwise we are groping and lost. At the same time it is and remains obvious that the church as a means in the hands of God, who is greater than she, exists for men and not men for a glorious church without spot or wrinkle. For us and for the people to whom we have to convey christianity, this whole church is merely the challenge to await the kingdom of God which is made known in the church, which is sacramentally present in the church, which begins in the church to take hold on the world: to await it in the completed and glorified form in which there will then be present the kingdom of God for whose coming we always pray in the "Our Father". This sense of the distinction between the kingdom of God and the church is part of the right relationship of man, of the christian and also of the priest, to his church.

3. *Mary*

God's salvation and his salvation-history are completely personalist. Salvation-history is carried on not by things, but by persons, by their freedom, their decision, and thus our relationship to the church is given shape in our relationship to Mary, who represents the true nature of the church in the purest form, and therefore represents the church herself. In Mary we see the completely redeemed person, the one who accepted in her own redemption the redemption of the world in flesh and spirit from God. In her we find those who have completely identified office and person. Her official position in salvation-history and her person absolutely coincide: she is purely the handmaid of the Lord for the salvation of the world. She has nothing else to do but surrender herself without reserve to God's decree and to accept what God gives to her and through her to the world: Jesus Christ, the Word made flesh. In him she is not and does not want to be anything but this pure disposition of God. In authentic official salvation history she is the holy one, the sinless one, the one who is filled with God's grace, the transfigured one, in fact the holy and blessed mother of God.

She is not merely a private individual who has made

good in her private life: she is an irremovable and necessary factor in God's plan of this salvation-history. We are therefore always sustained by what she did. What she did is also a factor in our situation in salvation history. Since we cannot and may not ever detach these objective personal realities from the persons, since we would otherwise lose any personal history of faith, hope and love, any dialogue, any genuine personal communion, and sink into a merely factual order, our association with Mary is really essential. Therefore devotion to Mary, built into and included within the wholeness of christian life, is something essential for the christian and particularly for the priest: something for which we can and should seek God's grace, in order really to possess, cherish and maintain this living personal relationship to Mary the mother of the Lord and thus our mother also.

Our priestly life is a life of the Spirit, for the Spirit, in the Spirit of the church, whom we find only there; at the same time – just as we distinguish between sacrament and sacramental grace – we can rightly distinguish between the church and her Holy Spirit, without separating these two, since they are definitely united through the permanent incarnation of the *Logos*, even though they are not identical. In this church we have a loving, priestly relationship to Mary, mother of the Lord.

24 LOVE

1. Foundation *and meditation on love*

First of all, some preliminary observations on this meditation (230–237). It is in an odd kind of way a parallel to the *Foundation*. Both seem to be a kind of philosophy: so much so that, so far as the nomenclature goes, we are talking here not of *caritas* but of *amor*. In reality, both are christian meditations belonging to the innermost area of revelation and only giving a kind of formal expression to this ultimate reality of christianity: this is not to suggest that the formal aspect could be separated from the reality which christianity reveals to man, but that it is certainly possible for man to perceive these ultimate basic structures in the diversity of the revealed christian reality, to bring them out more clearly and thus better to see, in the infinitely varied structures of the divinely established orders of nature and supernature, what is finally essential in salvation history.

The meditation on the *Foundation* and that on love tell us this almost in the same way, for both sum up the whole content of the *Exercises*. For this reason their place is outside the body of the *Exercises*. They are not a part, but the whole, and in fact two versions of the whole: at the beginning a kind of formal preview of the whole and in the meditation on love the whole as presented through the actual sequence of the *Exercises*, so that their real theme can be described by the final and definitive name which had hitherto been carefully avoided, the name of love. Therefore love, which dominated the whole of the *Exercises* from the very beginning (for otherwise the "more" of the *Foundation* itself would not have been possible), is here now really called love. Thus these two meditations – at the beginning and at the end of the *Exercises* – go together and this meditation on love again goes together with the whole of the *Exercises*. The decisive, the really important thing, the radically Ignatian element in the *Exercises* does not consist in theoretical truths which are put before us and considered. Nor even in a theological study translated into prayer; the *Exercises* take account of the immediacy of creator to creature, as was stated at the beginning.

2. *Immediacy of creator to creature*

This immediacy of the creature to God and of God to his creature, which substantially and decisively goes beyond what is merely essential, universally valid, always correct, is also that which comes to the fore and is realised in the election, the core of the *Exercises*: for there man asks about a will of God which he cannot adequately and unequivocally deduce from the objective norms of morality, even of supernaturally revealed christian morality. He wants to know how the living God in the immediacy of his relationship to me – in his Holy Spirit of course and not in any kind of philosophical relationship – deals with me.

This God and only God can say. That is why there are rules for the discernment of spirits (313–336) and times and methods for an election (169–188). In the election an immediacy between creature and creator becomes evident. This is conceived as possible, not in the rare case of some kind of mystic, but as something

presupposed and put before the retreatant to be practised; and the attempt at least is made to bring about
in us what Ignatius conceives as the relationship between God and creature and as source and foundation
of life, beyond all that is legal and calculable: a pure,
immediate mobility under God.

Love in the new testament sense is involved and presupposed throughout the whole of the *Exercises*. For this
love is not merely the reverential love of the creature
for its almighty Lord, not merely respect for the
structures of the world and of reality, because and in so
far as they are instituted by God, not merely a relationship to God mediated through the law and through
the world: it is a relationship to God in which God
offers himself as himself and I really look to God as he
is in himself, the greater God, the God elevated above
all the world, the God of the trinitarian life, the incarnate *Logos*. According to the teaching of the new
testament, this God imparts himself in love, he gives
himself, he makes us partakers of his divine nature
(2 Pet 1:4) and of his life, and we can therefore love
him in his own divine vitality, seclusion, unfathom-
ableness, unrelatedness; in himself, as he is in and for
himself.

This alone is love and this love, which is therefore
considered at the end, is clearly the inner reason and
foundation of all that happens in the *Exercises* as a
whole, when they are taken as *Exercises* directed to an
election. The election is not one in which we choose
something we see to be reasonable according to the
objective standards, but in which we are elected by God
and taken up into the pure encounter of his love for us,
which simply cannot any longer be given adequate

objective expression in anything other than God. The world, what we are ourselves, what we experience, what we can somehow evaluate as intellectual creatures, cannot tell us what God properly intends in our regard, because he really must bestow himself on us, as himself, as the immeasurable God who is subject to no criterion other than himself – of course in a wholly personal, peculiar way, conceived just for me and not for another. There is then only the election of being elected, the election of being called: an election which consists in hearing what God has decreed about me and indeed in a decree which is never again annulled by him, can never be given objective expression. The meditations on election properly so-called and the indifference described in the *Foundation* are directed to this.

It is a question really of direct love as it is understood in the new testament, of that seizure by the Holy Spirit which is not merely liberation from sin but also liberation from the aeons of this world, even in so far as they are good, even from the aeons of the law. All this is somehow surpassed in this immediacy of love of the creator for the creature. That is why the absolutely radical character of the *Exercises* as a whole – which is not generally understood – is now really made clear once again and acquires its proper name, as long of course as we understand what Ignatius means by love only in the light of the *Exercises* as a whole.

This love is that which was humbled in the first week. There I was told to consider the creature who is damned, so that I might to some extent remain in God's service if ever I were to forget his love. This love, granted to the creature as sinful, this love which the person has already once shut out, this love at whose

pure flame he knows the creature can rouse his deli-
berate hatred, his "No", this love which was so humbled and is aware of being the pure gift of God to
sinful man: this is the love which is the theme of this
meditation.

3. *Nature of this love*

In spite of the philosophical – one might almost say,
neoplatonic – touch, the theme of the meditation is
really God's love for me, to which I should respond
with the love made known to me through Jesus, a love
which man clearly sees in all its truth only by looking
to Jesus and his cross and to the risen one. This is so in
the first place because all the gifts which Ignatius asks
us to consider in the first part of the meditation on love
have in fact something ambiguous about them and
acquire their final, unequivocal meaning only through
Jesus Christ, when they are all – gifts of earthly life,
capacities, gifts also of the rest of nature – dissolved in
that really saving love which becomes conscious and is
conceived only in Jesus Christ. In a sense it might all be
a cruel trick of an infinite God who first of all allows us
to be of some account, only to make our fall more
terrible into the abyss of nothingness. Of course, from
the standpoint of pure metaphysics, we can always say
that God is good, God is holy, God is merciful. What
must this mean if the metaphysician can and must also
say it when he is in hell and although he is damned?
The love which truly saved us when we were sinners
and in spite of this, the love with which God loves the
world, sinful as it is, closed up against him, and there
loves us too: this love dawns upon us simply and solely
in Jesus Christ. Only from thence can we know that all

other good things in the world, in the gifts of nature and of grace, are real harbingers and elements of this divinely radical love which really saves and deifies.

To this extent it is true that this meditation on love – although it seems to range over the whole creation and the world, the whole of history and the whole extent of human experience in time and eternity – can see and know everything only through Christ, the incarnate Word, the eternal mercy of the Father, through the crucified one. This meditation on love is possible for the retreatant only after the fourth week. We must also say that the sinner's eye acquires the necessary clear-sightedness and light for this meditation on God in all things, God as infinite love in all things, only at the distance of indifference, resignation, freedom, often radical openness to God as he is in himself. But this freedom, which makes the world transparent and alone enables us to find God in the world, this indifference, is not what we have achieved by ourselves when it might have remained merely possible, but what has been gained only through the grace of God in Jesus Christ. It is only because the crucified one in his humanity, in absolute obedience, first created a distance from things as the sphere of an indifference, beyond all wordly reality, that I can now be indifferent at all and thereby possess that clear, penetrating vision in which I can discover this love of God for me in the world.

4. *Descending love*

This love (234, 237) is one which should bring about the descent of God. It sounds fine and it is also true to speak in theology of the return of creatures to God. But if this were the whole truth we should still have to say that we can really find God in virtue of the fact that God not only created the world but descended forever in his eternal Word into the world, although he is the God of inaccessible light; in his descent with his own reality, as *agape*, he has lost himself in his creation and never returns. Always remember that the immediacy of the beatific vision is presumably, to put it cautiously, really possible only in the incarnation and through the incarnation of the *Logos*: otherwise it would seem that the immediacy of vision in regard to the means – if it existed at all – would consume the knowing creature itself.

Do we not necessarily disappear to the extent that we come close to God? If this is not the case, why can we – who are creatures – settle down so to speak in the absolute, infinite, incomprehensible, consuming light of God himself? How is the creature, which is radically finite, also *capax infiniti*, capable of the infinite as such? Of course, as the infinite mystery of the incomprehensible God, but nevertheless known and experienced as incomprehensibility, as immediacy – how is anything of this kind possible at all? Ultimately, it can be possible only because God himself, without ceasing to be God, can give himself to the world; but this means at least, because the incarnation of the eternal *Logos* is the secularisation of God, God's going out of himself as *agape*, the basic truth and reality and possibility of God himself. It follows then that this love, which is so immediate to God that in his own life and in his glory he becomes the content of our creaturely life, this love is possible only because God himself has descended into this world. We conclude then that this ascending love which we have for God is always part of the realisation of God's descent into the world.

5. *Service*

If love then is possible only in and with the emptying
out of divine love into the world, and if this is the
essential structure of our love for God, then all this is
possible only through the kingdom of Christ as the
following of Christ, who is the *Logos* himself descending
into the world. We have to share in his lot, and thus in
actuality must also share in his passion, his love in the
sense in which it was considered during the third week.
But if such love is a sharing of the divine love for the
world in Jesus Christ, it is for that very reason necessarily a love of God in the world and in the church.
Therefore – as we are told in the meditations on love –
it becomes service.

This does not mean merely that we have to prove our
love in a crude sense, as if God could not also look into
our heart and could read the truth and reality of our
convictions only in the outward works; but our love, as
Ignatius says (since this very love of ours for God is the
"Yes" to his love of us), is essentially the acceptance of
this love. This love of God however is precisely the
descending love, imparting itself to the world, losing
itself so to speak in the world, the love which brings
about the incarnation of the *Logos*, which means the
abiding presence of the eternal *Logos* in his creature and
therefore also deified world and church. But anyone
who shares thus in the divine love descending into the
world, by accepting this divine love through his own
love, must himself try to realise his love also in this very
objectivation of the world. Such service is not an external proof of something which exists in its own nature
independently of this proof, but service with God in his

descent into the external, lost, sinful reality of this world, and therefore the love of which Ignatius speaks in this typical new testament sense is really not *eros* but *agape*. It is not a greedy poverty looking upwards, but the love already bestowed with divine glory and vitality and power which alone gives this *invenire deum in omnibus rebus* its true theological foundation.

6. *God in all things*

Why can we find God in everything? Because he has given himself to the world precisely as eternal glory and vitality, never to be confused with the world. This *quaerere et invenire deum in omnibus rebus* is not a philosophical truth and not a spiritual activity of a mind which simply experiences its transcendental character in the necessary mediation through what is finite and objective. Such a mind would merely have to transcend, would merely have to become indifferent. If one were so to speak merely a philosopher seeking God, it would be necessary continually to dissociate oneself from things, to be living in an ecstasy over against the world; or one would have to say that God is only to be known indirectly, the creator only to be perceived by savouring his finite gifts and seizing on these; and even then God would only be the one who was worshipped in silence as the infinitely distant horizon, remote and calm, before which religion must remain inarticulate.

The christian who shares in bringing about God's descent into the world, in bringing about this love of God for the world, the love in which God has accepted the world definitively for all eternity as his own innermost reality, as the utterance of himself, in spite of all distance, in spite of all crucifying death in Jesus Christ, such a christian in this love can love the world truthfully and radically in a way that would otherwise be impossible for man, and indeed not even conceivable. No one can turn to the world with so radical a love as he who does so in this descent of God, as he who has accepted forever and eternally in Jesus Christ the flesh of humanity and thus of the world, everything of course in its proper place and rank.

This love, therefore, as Ignatius describes it, goes out in service to the world; it is active, as required in the *Exercises*, whenever the question is raised: What must I do? It is active when we are called to make an effort with Christ. This love then looks away from itself; it does not forget itself; it is not so to speak a situation of mental introversion in which we are aware of ourselves, but we are aware of ourselves by forgetting ourselves in serving, working, striving, opening out, ministering to others. Because this love is not self-seeking, but seeks God and his world in which God in his love has lost himself, it is always ready to be transformed by God. Because it is not self-seeking and because this love then does not make love the criterion of all things, for the very reason that it is self-forgetting, it can always be content to let God be greater than anything else, greater even than itself. Therefore it can be and remain adoration, praise and power of the instrument serving the world's salvation. This love knows then that we come closer as the distance grows and that this is the paradoxical mystery of our relationship to God, that humility and love, distance and closeness, absolute submission to God's decree and our own reality, grow not in inverse ratio to one another but to the same degree.

7. *Love as "imago trinitatis"*

This love, as Ignatius sees it, is an *imago trinitatis*. We don't of course apply the powers of the soul in the same way that tools are applied externally to any kind of material to make something out of it. Ignatius is aware of the fact that this memory, understanding and will, form the *imago trinitatis*. If therefore here in the *Suscipe* he names this Trinity as present in human existence itself and if God bestows this *imago* in the final act of love, then what is meant here is a love which is itself sustained by the innermost mystery of the triune God in this self-realisation of the *imago trinitatis*, particularly since divine grace really creates a genuine special relationship to the three divine persons and is not merely a created objectivation of God's efficient causality, which would be the work *ad extra* of the one God.

If and in so far as grace means in the last resort uncreated grace – that is, God's self-communication to the created spirit – and if this self-communicating God is necessarily the triune God *as* triune, if in the beatific vision where this self-communication of God occurs we see the three divine persons as such and not merely a divine essence, then it is clear that this grace is promised as a trinitarian structure based on the *imago trinitatis* which we are. Hence this love as surrender of memory, understanding and will, which is practised throughout the *Exercises* as Ignatius conceived them, this love is the stirring of the *imago trinitatis* as such.

8. *The specifically Ignatian love*

The specific element of Ignatian love is really this "serving God in all things". Although immediacy to

God is essential to his spiritual teaching, Ignatius never thinks of by-passing the world, since everything can be a means, since the love which creates this immediacy is the love from and to God, descending in Christ through the church into the world; since therefore as such a love it carries out its redeeming and in this sense apostolic function.

For Ignatius, the person who has really acquired this indifference-dissociation in things is not yet at the goal, he is neither the platonic ecstatic nor the buddhist who has found his way to the nirvana of God's absoluteness through tearing down the veil of illusion: he is the man now who has received God's decree on what exactly and in the concrete has to be chosen in the world; the one who only through this indifference and as we might say through this crucifying death of his resignation is in a state to accept the worldly, the concrete, from God as the expression of his loving will and then to choose this.

Since in the last resort it is always a question of persons, this acceptance in fact means loving in the most truthful way. This love, then, in Ignatius' work, is really a love going out into the world, finding God in all things, so that God becomes mediator of our love for the world in his immediacy bestowed on us through his grace, and we do not merely find our way slowly through to God in a neoplatonic assent and then leave everything created behind us. No: we find God because he has sought and found us himself through his Holy Spirit in all immediacy. It is only in this way that he gives us this radical relationship to earthly reality itself, a relationship which can rest on the fact that it is promised us by God as the expression of his holy will, and therefore Ignatian man can be *in actione con-templativus*.

Of course, this is something which has come about through renunciation and mortification. Only in this way – as Ignatius continually insists – can all these things be means of rousing our devotion, since this pure stirring of love for God – in which alone I acquire my ultimate relationship to things – was given me by God or cannot exist at all unless man in a real renunciation, in a dying with Christ, has first broken away from his direct bondage to the things of the world. Anyone who has thus been promised this immediacy to creatures through the love of God, a God who himself is immediately present to us, can then really in principle find God in all things. This does not mean that we are then free to do as we like, but that we are absolutely ready to let God dispose of us and thus each time – according to God's sovereign will – to fall as it were divinely in love with certain things in the world.

Since God is Lord and creator of all things, since he willed everything in the world which has some sort of existence and meaning, it is clear from the first that God can send us to everything, that God himself can commit us to each and every thing, as he pleases; it is clear that there is no particular thing which is excluded from the first from possibly being what God can promise me in the immediacy of my love to him and his to me. It follows that this pure hovering – as we might describe it – in God's will over each particular thing, but also in readiness to each and every thing, the transcendence – if we may so put it – over every particular religious form, over every purely legal, purely regulated, fixed asceticism, is to be purely at God's disposal whether for maintaining possession of things or letting them go.

9. *The four points of the meditation*

The four points of the meditation throw light on each other. They are and must be understood from the first as interpenetrating factors of the one love for God and God's love for us, which demands the response of our love and indeed at each particular moment, corresponding to the living realisation of the *imago trinitatis* as love for his truth, for God as uncaused cause, and as love for the divine love, for the Holy Spirit. This love, then, is a love which finds its way through the concrete order of creation, of redemption, of my own reality as *individuum ineffabile* at any particular time. Only in this light do we understand the internal construction of the meditation.

You know of course that the exegetes are not agreed about the exact interpretation of these four points. Can we understand them as God's giving, as God's indwelling, as God's striving, and – so to speak – God's final descent into the world? Or are we to say that we first consider the various gifts of God and then God in the gifts, as he is *per praesentiam, per potentiam et per essentiam* (a form of meditation which is mentioned in a letter of Ignatius)? Or are we to say that God bestows his gifts, God is bestowed in his gifts in a personal presence, God bestows his gifts in personal activity and God bestows himself in these gifts? In the last resort, it all amounts to the same thing which is present in all four points: namely, finding God in all things, looking to God through all things, since the redeemed world and the redeemed subject are transparent to God and

God thus approaches us in all things. It is a question of sharing in the divinising and redeeming entry of God into all things and thus of freedom from egoism and love for the world in pure, loving surrender to this ever greater God.

With this love Ignatius lets the retreatant go out into the world. He means to send out someone who in this world finds God himself, who must never be confused with this world, not even with his most sacred gifts, not even with his objectivated will in the sacrament, in the religious life, in the service of souls. In comparison with all this he is the greater, and as this greater he is to be found in everything.

We might once again consider the priesthood from this aspect of love, for it is there emphasised that through the priesthood you are a distributor of God's gifts and receive them yourself so that God, the living God, who speaks in a personal way, places himself in you at the disposal of men: in your word, which is God's word and not yours, in the sacraments in which you are the ministers of God and servants of the work of his Christ. In your action too it is always God who is striving; and it is he who really imparts himself *per essentiam* in his uncreated grace in what you do and give to men. Thus priestly existence and activity are a concrete realisation of this love which always and entirely and in all things means his ineffable love for us: the greater God, the sublime God, the incomprehensible God, the God who is therefore somehow the crucifying God; the realisation also however of a love which finds this God in all things and naturally in the "things" into which God in his sovereign powers sends man.

10 *Suscipe*

When a deacon who is really called to the priesthood goes to the altar of ordination, he says: *Ecce adsum, mitte me*. Then in sacramental palpability and the truth of grace there takes place what really ought to take place in the meditations on election and here: namely, that the creature is absolutely open to the incomprehensible, infinite God, approaches him through grace, can himself share in the descent of God into the world.

We priests then must in fact understand this finding God in all things as concerned with those things for which God has freed, empowered and made possible our love: for love for men and precisely for that work which is entrusted to the priest. If we ask in which things we can find God, if in the last resort all that matters is to find God, we can say quite simply: in our priestly life. Here we are close to God, here we are close to the creature made divine, here we utter the word of God, here we dispense God's mysteries, here we work with him and his Christ for the salvation of the world, here we are servants of the church, in all this we are enabled to find God in all things.

If a deacon at the altar of ordination says, *Adsum*, we can also say here with Ignatius, *Suscipe*: Take me with all that I am, with that deepest root of my nature which is called freedom, with the *imago trinitatis*, which has become the true likeness and realisation of the divine *Logos* in grace. Here I am with all that I am and have, with my life, with my power, with my time, with what I cannot foretell in my life. Everything has already been surrendered to God. *Suscipe* and *adsum*. The ultimate meaning of the *Exercises* and the ultimate meaning of what happens on the day of ordination to the priesthood is the same: God loves me and I can love him. I love him because he has given me the power to love him and therein I have finally lost myself in God.